I0153454

Reestablishing
America's
Global Power

JOHN UBALDI

DocUmeant *Publishing*
244 5th Avenue
Suite G-200
NY, NY 10001
646-233-4366
www.DocUmeantPublishing.com

Published by
 DocUmeant Publishing
244 5th Avenue, Suite G-200
NY, NY 10001
646-233-4366

© 2025 John Ubaldi. All rights reserved.

No part of this book may be reproduced in any form or by any electronic
or mechanical means, including information storage and retrieval systems,
without permission in writing from the publisher, except by a reviewer who
may quote brief passages in a review.

The publisher has used its best efforts in preparing this book, and the
information provided herein is provided "as is".

The views expressed in this book are solely those of the author and do not
necessarily reflect the views of the publisher.

The author has attempted to recreate events, locales, and conversations from
their memories of them. Some names and identifying details may have been
changed to protect the privacy of individuals.

Editor Anne C. Jacob of Popin Edits
AnneCJacob.com

Cover & Book design and production by Ginger Marks of
DocUmeant Designs
DocUmeantDesigns.com

Library of Congress Control Number: 2025937813
ISBN: 9781957832685 (pbk)
ISBN: 9781957832692 (epub)

Contents

Acknowledgements

This book is dedicated to my parents who instilled in their children the greatness of America and benefits the United States has bequeathed to the world and continues to do so. I would also like to dedicate this book to all the members of the US Armed Forces who have served or are currently serving their country, but especially to those individuals who gave the ultimate sacrifice, their lives on the altar of freedom! As it is often stated, "All gave some, but some gave all!" Let us never forget their sacrifice!

Introduction

The disastrous Afghanistan withdrawal should have been a wake-up call that American foreign policy has been one adjunct failure since the end of the Cold War, with each Democrat and Republican administration reacting to events instead of incorporating a comprehensive national security strategy.

Far too often, both Democrats and Republican administrations have failed to incorporate all elements of US national executive agencies into a comprehensive national security strategy for the post-Cold War world, and it's imperative that we need one for the twenty-first century.

With this lack of strategy, is it any wonder the American people are confused about the role the US plays on the international stage? As the US has massive challenges here at home, we are seeing billions sent abroad. The American people don't see the correlation between what transpires globally and its impact on the United States, because our elected officials have failed to make this connection.

The intent of this book is not that everyone or anyone who reads this will accept or agree with everything written, but the purpose is to begin the dialogue to address the multitude of complex and challenging issues confronting the United States America.

America is facing a multitude of challenges domestically as well as internationally, with the country facing over $36 trillion national debt, which, if left unchecked, will leave future generations saddled with dismal economic choices. The greatest challenge America faces and one neither party wants to address or admit is that the nation's entitlement programs of Social Security, Medicare, and Medicaid are going broke. If not addressed, these programs will become insolvent in less than nine years, leaving nationally elected officials with only three choices: to raise massive taxes or to massively reduce benefits, or a combination of both.

Not addressing America's fiscal situation will prevent the US from engaging and being the leader of the free world, as more dominant powers will seek to lay claim to global leadership abdicated by the United States. In this case, it is China who is trying to dethrone the US, and does anyone believe Beijing will adhere to Democratic principles?

The Bretton Woods system, put forth by the United States, "initially envisioned a system of rules, institutions, and procedures to regulate international commerce and monetary systems. This led to promoting the establishment of three major institutions: the International Monetary Fund (IMF), the World Bank (then called the International Bank for Reconstruction and Development), and the International Trade Organization, which would set rules and adjudicate disputes, thereby promoting expanded global trade."[1]

Does anyone believe China will become the force for global stability and economic liberalization that has been the hallmark of the liberal economic order since the United States instituted the Brenton Woods system during the waning days of World War II?

America must begin by getting its fiscal house in order, but for the United States to compete and to be the global leader in innovation against rising powers such as China, America needs a top tier educational system. The greatest Civil Rights issue of our time is America's dysfunctional educational system! COVID-19 ripped the band-aid off America's chronic failing educational system, one which we will discuss in greater depth in subsequent chapters.

In 2023, an article in Scientific American stated that only one-third of students were able to read fluently, and 40 percent could not read. Currently, half of all American school children enrolled in the nation's K-12 public school system can't read or do math to grade level.[2] In Spring of 2021, Lauren Bushnell pointed out that math and reading deficiencies are greater among black and Hispanic children than those of their white peers. Among the ethnic minorities over 70% of black and Hispanic children are deficient at grade level in math and English.[3] If America is to compete on the global stage and remain the innovation leader; we will need a viable top tier educational system

America faces enormous challenges internationally, one that the US hasn't faced since World War II. The United States faces an aggressive China, who wants nothing better than to supplant the United States as the world's dominant power. If this wasn't challenging enough, the US faces an expansionist Russia, under President Vladamir Putin, who is trying to revive the old Russian empire. This beginning phase was done by Russian forces invading Ukraine.

> Russia's invasion of Ukraine forced Washington to rethink its fundamental assumptions about Moscow. Every US president from Bill Clinton to Joe Biden had sought some degree of engagement with Russia. As late as 2021, Biden expressed hope that Russia and the United States could arrive at "a stable, predictable relationship." But Russia's brutal war on Ukraine has radically altered that assessment. It is now clear that the two countries will remain antagonists for years to come. The Kremlin possesses immense disruptive global power and is willing to take great risks to advance its geopolitical agenda. Coping with Russia will demand a long-term strategy, one that echoes containment, which guided the United States through the Cold War, or what President John F. Kennedy called a "long, twilight struggle" against the Soviet Union.[4]

Iran is filling the vacuum left by the perception the US is abandoning the region and is now expanding the chaos throughout the Middle East, as all three of these nations have virtually formed the twenty-first century version of the axis powers of World War II.

We are witnessing a perception by our adversaries who view America as a diminished superpower. This scenario is being played out, as America lost its deterrence, and no one fears the United States. This lack of credibility only emboldens America's adversaries. Even our allies are concerned about this lack of deterrence and are worried about America's staying power. The botched Afghan withdrawal further cemented this perception as the world witnessed firsthand how the US abandoned our allies without any notice of American pullout from the country.

Now China's stated goal is to supplant the US as the new global superpower, and the disastrous and chaotic Afghan withdrawal crystallized in the eyes of the world, especially or adversaries that America is in decline. This perception was seen by Russia as American weakness, and many believe this led to the invasion of Ukraine by Russia. Russia and others capitalized as they didn't fear any retribution by the United States.

The real problem with US foreign policy is that it dramatically changes every four or eight years with different Republican and Democratic administrations. But this is never more evident than with the Trump administration. President Trump has changed the dynamics of US foreign policy and has taken an America first approach, which has repudiated past Democratic and Republican global strategies.

From the beginning of the Cold War in the late 1940s until the collapse of former Soviet Union in 1992, the stated policy was a containment strategy which was put forth by a State Department official named Geoge Kennan serving in Moscow.

> George F. Kennan authored the concept of containment, according to which the United States should "contain" Soviet expansionism but should not use, or threaten to use, force to remove the communist regime. Kennan first raised the idea in what became known as "The Long Telegram," sent on February 22, 1946. It recommended a US policy based on the tenet that the Soviet system would not cooperate with the United States and, furthermore, had to act as an enemy to preserve its own power.[5]

This containment strategy had become the stated policy of both Republican and Democratic administrations for the next forty years until the final collapse of the Soviet Union.

With the end of the Cold War, the United States emerged as the world's only hegemonic power and with this newfound leadership, America failed to articulate a new global strategy in a post-Cold War era. Since then, each new administration, whether they be Democrat or Republican failed to articulate a global strategy, instead came into office wanting to focus on domestic priorities.

Former National Security Advisor Zbigniew Brezinski in the Carter administration was aware of this when he wrote *The Grand Chessboard* in 1997.

It's ironic that the scenario Brezinski feared the most is transpiring as we speak, with China, Russia, and Iran coalescing, not by ideology, but at a chance to reshape the global world order away from the system set up by the US after the Second World War. It would be eerily similar to the scale and scope to the Sino-Soviet bloc, but this time, instead of Russia as the dominate power, China would be the center, Russia would be the follower, and Iran would be the junior partner—all with the same grievance of curtailing America's global power base.[6]

In each case, the newly elected president campaigned on repudiating the foreign policy of the previous administration, and political partisanship also factored into the equation always championing their party's president and criticizing the other's party's president. This was never more apparent than during the wars in Iraq and Afghanistan.

Since the end of the Cold War, continuing into the war on terror, America failed to utilize all elements of its national power with virtually no foreign policy direction from either Democrat or Republican administrations. Although Vice President Kamala Harris did not mention global affairs or international policy, these were prominent discussion points in President Trump's campaign. The events of the September 11 terror attack catapulted the US into twenty years of perpetual conflict throughout the greater Middle East, one with which most Democrats and Republicans supported.

With the end of the Cold War, but after September 11, the Defense Department took the lead in conducting and implementing US foreign policy, with the State Department taking a back seat.

Each president who came into office approached the presidency with no strategic plan, and never articulated what role the US would play in global affairs. Failure on both points forced the United States to be involved, first in the Balkans, then after September 11, in the Middle East. Both Democratic and Republican presidents always had the US reacting to events instead of being proactive.

Both Democratic and Republican presidents failed to heed the wise counsel of British Prime Minister Winston Churchill, whose statement on the beginning of the start of a war is often quoted: "Never, never, never believe any war will be smooth and easy, or that anyone who embarks on that strange voyage can measure the tides and hurricanes he will encounter. The Statesman who yields to war fever must realize that once the signal is given, he is no longer the Master of Policy but the slave of unforeseeable and uncontrollable events."

During the presidency of President Joe Biden, the administration's national defense strategy has long been an overview with few specifics, devoid of any strategic direction. In fairness, previous administrations, whether Republican or Democrats, never put forth a full national security strategy. Now considering the immense challenges confronting the United States, presidents of both political parties after the end of the Cold War have not articulated, nor have they explained to the American people what America's unique role in the world is.

The economy is the number one issue on the minds of Americans. This was never more evident than how voters cast their ballots during the 2024 presidential election. Due to economic uncertainty at home, the American people were reluctant to keep providing economic resources abroad, especially continued funding to Ukraine in its ongoing fight against Russia.

With America facing over a $36 trillion national debt, the time is at hand to reorganize and reform all federal government agencies to strengthen America's national security. We will discuss more of this in Chapter one — how the greatest national security threat to the United States is not from China, Russia, or international terrorism, but from America's national debt which, if not addressed, will severely harm America's economic viability. By not fully coming to grips with America's exploding national debt, it gravely threatens America's national security and will have global implications.

Democrats consistently believe the way forward is to raise taxes on the wealthy, with their often-repeated moniker of "making the wealthy pay their fair share," accompanied by a sharp reduction in national defense, coupled with massive government spending on social programs. Republicans focus more on reducing domestic spending, with lowering taxes, but neither party, until now, has focused on reforming all US federal agencies.

Since the end of the Cold War, but especially after the wars in Iraq and Afghanistan, there has been no meaningful discussion describing the future goals of the Department of Defense, the US Department of State, or overhauling US intelligence for the new challenges that America faces in the twenty-first century.

With America confronting challenges from near peer competitors such as Russia, but especially China, America needs to integrate all executive agencies into US National Security, and this begins with a vibrant and innovative US economy. The United States, if it's to remain the innovation leader and be able to compete globally, needs a robust and top-tier educational system at the K-12 level and in post-secondary education. Right now, America's K-12 system is a dysfunctional disaster.

America's national security is threatened without a top-tier educational system, and if America is to compete in the "new frontier" of space to outpace the Chinese who are actively challenging America, the US needs an educated population.

America needs to incorporate how the Department of Commerce and Labor integrates into our National Security by establishing a robust manufacturing base. As we saw during the COVID-19 crisis, American manufacturing has been outsourced to China and other countries around the world. A new challenge that we're facing is cybersecurity. Many companies, entities, and government departments and agencies have been attacked by cyber security actors around the world, including Russia and China.

Various questions need to be addressed, and energy security is one key issue that directly impacts national security. Americans voted overwhelmingly for President Donald Trump, who has vowed to make energy independence one of his top priorities. Other issues, such as immigration, are also being addressed. The Biden Administration removed all border safeguards, allowing up to ten million illegal migrants to enter the US, with many coming from counties hostile to the US. Of the illegals who have entered, hundreds have been apprehended who are on the terror watch list.

The question remaining is, how many that the US has no knowledge or visibility of have entered?

Neither Democrat nor Republican administrations have ever given a clear definition of how all the federal agencies are integrated into the nation's national security strategy, with little or no discussion on major reforms of the national executive agencies. For example, what are the future force plans for the Department of Defense? How is the Pentagon reshaping its strategy in dealing with China in the event that China decides to invade or conduct a naval blockade of Taiwan? How will the Trump administration rebuild America's industrial defense base?

With his new administration, President Donald Trump is facing a far different world in 2025 than the one when he left office in 2021. The chaotic withdrawal by the United States has done more harm to US global standing, with many believing this was the impetus Russian President Vladamir Putin needed to invade Ukraine. America was once again weak. Putin remembered how the Obama administration allowed him to get away with anything he wanted, and most of that administration had been advising President Biden, and this would include Biden himself who served as President Obama's Vice President.

President Trump faces challenges domestically as well as globally, and the decisions he makes will re-shape the United States for decades to come.

One

America's Greatest National Security Threat

America is facing its greatest national security threat and one that is not coming from China, nor from Russia or Iran, but from its ballooning national debt! Right now, the national debt has crossed $36 trillion, and if not addressed, will severely impact the nation's economic viability into the future. Failure to tackle America's debt crisis will cripple America's national security, make the world less safe, and severely impact the security of the United States.

All during the 2024 presidential campaign, the candidates vying for the presidency neither discussed nor were asked by the mainstream media how their economic plans would begin to address America's national debt.

In an address to the Congress on January 25, 1983, Ronald Reagan stated, "A strong American economy is essential to the well-being of our country and security of our friends and allies." Presidents from both political parties, whether Republican or Democratic administrations, placed us on this unsustainable path with endless wars that weren't funded and misguided domestic programs that were badly financed, further saddling the country with uncontrollable national debt.

From 2021 to 2024, interest rates went to a forty-year high, and the interest in financing that debt went up as well. As of this writing, interest payments are well over a trillion dollars, surpassing what the nation allocates for national defense and more than the entitlement programs of Social Security, Medicare, and Medicaid.

Just before his retirement in 2011, Chairman of the Joint Chiefs of Staff Admiral Michael Mullen was asked at a symposium, "What is America's greatest national security threat?" His response stunned many in attendance, expecting him to say international terrorism, as we were still involved with the wars in Iraq and Afghanistan. Many thought he would state it was Russia, or China, which was then becoming a troubling concern for the US. Instead, he commented that the greatest national security threat the United States faces is the nation's unsustainable national debt.

Speaking before a Senate Appropriations Subcommittee on Defense, Admiral Michael Mullen stated:

> As we look to our military's posture and budget, we recognize that our country is still reeling from a grave and global economic downturn and is maintaining nearly historic fiscal deficits and national debt. Indeed, I believe that our debt is the greatest threat to our national security. If we as a country do not address our fiscal imbalances in the near-term, our national power will erode. Our ability to respond to crises and to maintain and sustain influence will diminish.

Our national economic health is creating real budgetary pressures. For too much of the past decade we have not been forced to be fully disciplined with our choices. But for the foreseeable future, cost will be a critical element of nearly every decision we face. We must now carefully and deliberately balance the imperatives of a constrained budget environment with the requirements we place on our military in sustaining and enhancing our security. We must identify areas where we can reduce spending while minimizing risk. This will affect our posture, force structure, modernization efforts, and compensation and benefits. The Defense Department must and will become more efficient and disciplined, while simultaneously improving our effectiveness.[7]

This was also echoed by Robert Gates, then the Secretary of Defense under Barack Obama, and who had served under President George W. Bush, when Secretary Gates gave a farewell address mentioning America's national debt is going to be an issue the US will have to confront. Europe will have to understand that the American people are going to want to know why we are spending money defending Europe when the US has its own domestic challenges. Especially if Europe is unwilling to take care of their own security.

Secretary Gates, addressing the *Atlantic Council*, stated:

> Let me conclude with some thoughts about the political context in which all of us must operate. As you all know, America's serious fiscal situation is now putting pressure on our defense budget, and we are in a process of assessing where the U.S. can or cannot accept more risk as a result of reducing the size of our military. Tough choices lie ahead, affecting every part of our government, and during such times, scrutiny inevitably falls on the cost of overseas commitments—from foreign assistance to military basing, support, and guarantees.

> The blunt reality is that there will be dwindling appetite and patience in the U.S. Congress—and in the American body politic writ large—to expend increasingly precious funds on behalf of nations that are apparently unwilling to devote the necessary resources or make the necessary changes to be serious and capable partners in their own defense. Nations apparently willing and eager for American taxpayers to assume the growing security burden left by reductions in European defense budgets.

Indeed, if current trends in the decline of European defense capabilities are not halted and reversed, Future U.S. political leaders–those for whom the Cold War was not the formative experience that it was for me – may not consider the return on America's investment in NATO worth the cost.[8]

At the time when both Gates and Mullen made their statements, the national debt was a staggering $14 trillion, now it's $36 trillion and growing rapidly. When President Biden assumed the presidency in 2021, the national debt was $28 trillion, now it just passed $36 trillion.

Both political parties often talk of reducing the national debt, but never place rhetoric with actual specific policies in reducing America's insatiable appetite for spending. Both parties have different approaches to achieving debt reduction, with Democrats believing in higher taxes and a sharp reduction in Defense spending, with Republicans favoring tax cuts to spur economic growth, coupled with sharp reductions in domestic spending. Both fail to address the third rail of politics and that is entitlement spending. This would include Social Security, Medicare, and Medicaid.

Nobody wants to admit it, but most of the national debt is tied up in entitlement spending related to Social Security, Medicare, and Medicaid, as this has always been the third rail of American politics anybody whoever even talks about touching these programs is a sure loser as the voters will make them pay at the ballot box.

When dealing with the US federal budget, it is important to understand the difference between two distinct aspects of the budgetary process: non-discretionary and discretionary spending. With one, you are able to make yearly reductions or increases in prospective appropriations. With the other, alterations can only be made by changing the existing law. Non-discretionary spending is allocated for items that are non-essential, and it can be increased or decreased through the appropriations process. Discretionary spending, also called mandatory spending, is not subjected to through the normal appropriations process and can only be changed through legislation. This includes Social Security, Medicare, and Medicaid. Mandatory spending equals roughly over 60 percent of the US federal budget, leaving Congress and the President to haggle over the other 40 percent, because neither side wants to deal with reforming Social Security, Medicare, and Medicaid. Incidentally, all will be insolvent in just over ten years.[9]

The non-discretionary spending can only be expanded or reduced by Congress each year, but changes to discretionary spending such as entitlement spending, which encompasses Social Security, Medicare, and Medicaid, can only be done by changing the law itself of the existing programs. No one of either party is willing to do this, instead using it as a political weapon to attack the other party for not taking care of seniors.

A great example of this scenario played out when President Barack Obama placed former White House Chief of Staff to President Bill Clinton, Erskine Bowles, to lead Obama's National Commission on Fiscal Responsibility and Reform, co-chaired with former Republican Senator from Wyoming, Alan Simpson. Bowles was congratulated by his ninety-year-old Mother, but she also firmly reiterated, "Leave Social Security alone!"

It's time for our public leaders to finally address this looming debt bomb by leveling with the American people how Social Security is funded and administered. Far too many people across the country are badly misinformed about Social Security, with many believing that there is an account with their name on it set aside waiting for them to access the account upon retirement.

Social Security was intended to be a supplemental retirement system, to give added retirement funding to individuals. Instead, it morphed into Americans' sole source of retirement. What many Americans fail to understand about Social Security is that it is funded by current workers through payroll taxes that the employee and employer pay into the Social Security Trust. With the establishment of Social Security in the mid-1930's, it was set up as a pay as go system, where current workers pay for those who are currently retired. At the time of the establishment of Social Security, the ratio was sixty workers for one retiree, then it dropped to thirty to one. Now, it hovers around two workers for every one retiree. The Social Security and Medicare Actuary and the Congressional Budget Office (CBO) have issued numerous reports, indicating if nothing is done to address the problem, Social Security will run out of funds in 2033, and Medicare will be insolvent in 2036.

Addressing a Senate Committee on the Budget, The Congressional Budget Office's Chief of Long-Term Analysis, Molly Dahl reported that Social Security faces a significant financial challenge in the coming decade. The program is financed by revenues from payroll taxes and from income taxes on Social Security benefits; those revenues are credited to the Old-Age and Survivors Insurance (OASI) Trust Fund and the Disability Insurance (DI) Trust Fund. The Congressional Budget Office projects that starting in a decade,

Social Security's revenues will not be sufficient to cover all the benefits that are due under current law.

Medicare is funded in two parts: Medicare Part A and Part B. Medicare Part A is funded mainly through the Hospital Insurance (HI) payroll tax, which is levied on both employers and employees.

> Employees pay a 1.45% tax on wage earnings below the threshold of $200,000 ($250,000 for married couples) and a 2.35% tax on wages exceeding the threshold. Employers pay a tax equal to 1.45% of employees' earnings. Payroll taxes accounted for 89% of Part A revenue in 2022. An additional 8% of revenues came from income taxes on Social Security benefits received by high-income beneficiaries. In contrast, beneficiaries must pay premiums to enroll in Medicare Parts B and D, but premium revenues cover only about one quarter of expenses. Nearly all the remainder is covered by general revenues. Medicare Advantage is paid for by a combination of funds allocated to Medicare Parts A and B. In 2022, Medicare Advantage expenses accounted for 49% of Medicare Part A spending.[10]

Whoever assumes the presidency in 2033 and whoever is serving in Congress will only have three options, substantially raise taxes or substantially cut benefits or a combination of both, and neither of these options is plausible, as our political leaders have failed to do anything about this looming crisis.

The US federal government is not only drowning in debt caused by reckless spending. This fiscal disease has also spread into many of our most populus states, such as California, which boasts the world's fifth largest economy. Behind the glitz and glamor of the golden state is an entirely different economic picture! California, for all its wealth, portends a very different economic situation for the vast citizenry of the state. California has the dubious distinction of having one of the highest unemployment rates in the country, the largest income inequality, and the largest homeless population, despite spending billions with little to show for it. California ranks as one of the most anti-business climates in the country, with the highest tax rate, the highest sales tax, with one of the worst road infrastructures in the country, ranks near the bottom in educational achievement.

Just examine how the state and local government handled the Los Angeles fires. With the highest sales tax, gas tax, and income tax in the country, the state's failing infrastructure and poor mismanagement by government leaders was a great contributing factor in the devastation which occurred.

For all the clamor of how they are the most equitable as it relates to ethnic minorities, only 25 percent of black and Hispanic children in the California school system can read or do math to grade level. For all public-school children, only about half are reading or doing math at grade level. It's also interesting how with the failing public school system in California Democratic Governor Gavin Newsom sends his four children to a $60,000 dollar a year private school in the wealthy enclave of Ross, located in Marin County, one of the wealthiest counties in the country. Even during the COVID-19 pandemic, Newsom's children attended a private school for in-person learning, while six million public school children were forced to learn via Zoom for two years. Many of the most vulnerable children lost precious learning time, from which they will never recover from.

Examine California's finances. Just two short years ago, the state made a $165 billion revenue error calculating a short-term spike in income taxes, by projecting emanating from the state's three largest sources would indefinitely be and remain over $200 billion. Governor Gavin Newsom declared his state had a $97 billion surplus. And in fiscal 2022-23 the budget peaked at $300 billion. Instead of prudent fiscal spending, the state went on a spending binge and allocated new spending on health/welfare programs and cash payments to low-income families. Newsom and California based the budget on wildly faulty assumptions that massive amounts of federal funding from the COVID-19 pandemic would continue indefinitely. Unfortunately for the state of California, revenues dissipated, and the state was faced with close to a $73 billion deficit which was papered over utilizing budget gimmicks, borrowing, tapping into emergency reserves, and faulty assumptions of future spending reductions.

Upon leaving office after being termed out in 2026, California's Democratic Governor Gavin Newsom will bequeath to his successor a state in a fiscal disaster. California's Legislative Analyst, Gabriel Petek, projected operating budget deficits into double digits for the foreseeable future. With the wildfires that have ravaged the Los Angeles region, it is interesting to note that on page eight of Petek's report, he makes an ominous reference to the lack of funding for disasters.[11]

> Outside of government and health care, the state has added no jobs in a year and a half. Similarly, the number of Californians who are unemployed is 25 percent higher than during the strong labor markets of 2019 and 2022. Consumer spending (measured by inflation adjusted retail sales and taxable sales) has continued to decline throughout 2024.[12]

This spiraling of California's economy was decades in the making. California's environmental regulators were also piling on demands that made California's factories even less able to compete. A good example was the General Motors plant in Los Angles which made the popular Firebirds, one the of the signature vehicles for GM. The red paint used that gave the Firebird its unique shiny finish required more solvents to achieve its custom glow. California's air regulators gave GM an ultimatum — if you want to stay in business you have to stop utilizing the solvent. Various companies, including General Motors, faced undue burdensome regulations and taxes. They decided to either move to another business-friendly state or close their manufacturing plants down, thereby laying off thousands of well-paying union jobs.

Many businesses complain of the excessive anti-business climate which is pervasive throughout the golden state. State leaders often use broad brushes to paint their version of how these companies should do business. However, the vast majority of elected officials running the state have never run a business and only come into office from academia, government, or non-profits. This was on full display as $25 billion over the past five years was doled out by California to various agencies to deal with the homeless crisis. The state could not account for how the $25 billion was spent, or where it went. The end result was that California experienced more homelessness.

The vast amount of job growth in California is centered on lower-paying service industries, and the job growth that is created is in government employment, which does not generate its own wealth, but depends on tax receipts from the citizens of California.

Much of the growth in the US is centered in the Midwest, the south, and in the Carolinas, with the often-maligned red states of Florida and Texas booming and having a government budget surplus.

What has California gained? One could make the argument that the golden state leads the world in renewable energy and electric vehicle ownership. But its industrial and manufacturing sectors have been decimated, and it boasts the highest housing, transportation, and electricity costs in the country. Its climate accomplishments are illusory, a product of deindustrialization, high energy costs, and, more recently and improbably, depopulation. California's push for its green agenda and anti-business climate has only led the golden state to have the highest income inequality of any state in the US. This has led to the poor becoming even poorer and placed the minority communities back into segregated housing at numbers not seen since the 1960s.[13]

California's policies have decimated and are continuing to devastate the manufacturing, logistics, transportation, and agriculture sectors, where many of the well-paying jobs from the middle class are centered. Most of the jobs created pay roughly less than $45,000 a year. This makes it very difficult to live in one of the highest cost-of-living states in the country. It's a wonder California leads the nation in out-migration to other low-cost states, such as Texas and Florida.

For the blue-collar, middle-class, and the poor, life in California is hardly golden, but a land of misery. and a new term, which has been coined by Jennifer Hernandez of *The Breakthrough Institute*. The new "Green Jim Crow" era has been embedded in the once proud Golden State.

Just examine the Golden state's financial situation. The Reason Foundation's Mariana Trujillo wrote that California was used to be the state everyone looked to for economic growth, but now the once- proud golden state has the highest long-term debt burden, when you include state and the various local governments, which has surged to well over a half a trillion dollars, making its debt obligations the highest in the US.[14]

The financial situation in California is a fiscal disaster. Remember, only two short years ago, the state bragged about having the highest state surplus in the country at $97 billion. Unfortunately, the state based its number on faulty data, although the California's Legislative Analyst Office warned state leaders this surplus was reflective of federal funding for COVID-19. Instead of shoring up its fiscal liabilities and paying down past debt, the state went on a spending binge, and now they are facing annual budget deficits of $30 billion. Currently, the state is begging Washington for a $40 billion bailout out to assist in helping with the massive wildfire damage in Loas Angeles. Despite all this, the state continues to bleed money, paying out $9 billion to cover illegal immigrants' healthcare costs.

Trujillo continued to highlight the fact that the golden state is bleeding revenue with one of the worst debt ratios in the country. With all its vast wealth generated mainly from Silicon Valley technology companies, California owes vast sums of money, with little revenue coming into the state. For years, the States's Legislative Analyst office has repeatedly warned elected officials about this debt crisis all to no avail. Far too often, the state has relied on the top one percent to pay all the services the state pays out. When this group does well on Wall Street, the state is flush with revenue, but when Wall Street enters a bear market, revenues from the top one percent drop precipitously. Now the state will be facing multi-billion-dollar deficits for the foreseeable future.[15]

The fiscal crisis in California is not just confined to the golden state. It has infected many other states. By adopting California's disastrous economic model, they are facing the same results and greatly hampering the US from expanding economically. By all measures, California should lead the nation in economic growth like it has been in the past. Instead, it languishes at the bottom in economic viability, especially for the middle class and low-income earners. For many, California has been facing a crisis for decades. The problem is the way California is set up financially, with its progressive tax system.

In essence, it means California taxes the top one percent to pay for almost all its state revenue. Almost fifty percent of all taxes in California are paid by the top one percent. The top five percent pay almost eighty to ninety percent of all taxes in that state. The real problem for California, and the other states mentioned earlier, is that they over-promise benefits that were not properly funded and not properly set up for the future. Many of the states have wasted hundreds of billions of dollars on programs, which failed to meet expectations and had little or no oversite.

For example, in California's massive government bureaucracy, unfunded health and pensions are severely inadequate to cover the benefits promised. Beginning in the late 1990s, Democratic Governor Gray Davis, with pressure from California Public Employees' Retirement System (CalPERS), insisted benefits could be increased, because budget surpluses had been forecasted as far as the eye could see. Within two years, recession crippled state finances. Revenues massively dropped and the budget went deep into the red. Since that time, California has faced a boom-and-bust budgetary cycle. When the stock market does well, the state is flush with revenue, but when the markets retract as we have seen in the past few years, revenues generated by the top 1 percent drop significantly, and the state feels economic pain.

California's progressive tax system functions on the basis that the top 1 percent pay the vast majority of the taxes. When the financial markets do well, the state is flush with revenue from the wealthiest Californians. However, when the financial markets retract, these same individuals' investments retract, and this means less revenue to the state. Unfortunately, California's political leaders spend like drunken sailors during the boom years, then face severe cuts during the lean years, but many of the programs are locked in and can't be cut except by vote by the legislature. With the Democratic Party's total control of all levers of power, their only answer is more taxes and more regulations of business. This has forced many businesses to move to greener pastures found in states like Florida and Texas.

The same situation has impacted their unemployment insurance system. Prior to the recession of 2008–9, California gave out generous benefits, didn't properly fund them, and went into debt. The federal government provided a loan to the state to cover the shortfall. California took years to pay it back, but during the pandemic, had to borrow billions from Washington, which hasn't been paid back. This situation was made worse by a $30 billion scheme of fraudulent unemployment payments during the

COVID-19 pandemic. The state's unemployment system is broken. If they have another recession, they will be unable to meet demand from unemployment insurance. California still has a huge benefit problem where there are more benefits to going out than coming in.

California is not the only state to face the economic calamity of short-sighted political decisions. Illinois is also facing a dire financial situation, one of its own making. Poor political economic decisions of the past decades have placed the state billions of dollars in debt. Illinois keeps making disastrous economic decisions that burden the state with one of the highest state and local tax rates in the country. Instead of prosperity, it has only led to hundreds of thousands of its residents and businesses fleeing to states with less of a tax burden.[16]

New York, which prides itself on its effectiveness, is often at odds with red states, such as Texas and Florida. However, New York's economic situation is far from rosy. The state faces a cumulative three-year budget gap of $13.9 billion, which was forecasted by the state's Division of the Budget (DOB) and put forth in a report by the State Comptroller Thomas P. DiNapoli for the fiscal year of 2024-25. DiNapoli stated in his report that New York needed to get a handle on spending and revenues, coupled with understanding the myriad of challenges that the state finances will face with regard to economic competitiveness, and how the state moves forward in the years to come.[17]

Many of the New England states are in the same position as California. New York and Illinois are facing massive debt problems. The difference between the states and the federal government is that the federal government doesn't have to balance its budget. States have a legal obligation inside their constitution to have a yearly balanced budget. Many of the problems the various states face are self-inflicted. Over-generous health and pension benefits to public sector workers were never properly funded over the long term, and massive government spending on various programs was locked into place. These were purposely done to appease various core constituencies.

The main reason to mention the dismal economic situations of many of the states, as these are the largest and most populus, and if they face a fiscal crisis, it will be an anchor around the neck of

America economically and will further hamper economic growth. Currently, many of these states are losing individuals to more prosperous regions such as Texas, Florida, the costal Carolinas, and various mid-west states. All these states have a pro-business climate, minimal state income taxes, or none. Instead of the high taxes, high regulations, and anti-business climate prevalent in the states mentioned.

Far too often, throughout our public discourse, we hear the rhetoric that the wealthy are not paying their fair share of tax, and many blame the Trump tax cuts of 2017 for further raising the national debt. This has always been a false assumption, not based on factual information.

In a report by the House Ways and Means Committee, Chairman Republican Jason Smith stated:

> While the Congressional Budget Office provides a valuable service to the Congress, its track record in predicting the economic and fiscal outcome of the 2017 Trump tax cuts is poor, to say the least. It's troubling that the CBO issued a report intended to help policymakers make decisions about future legislative initiatives without ever asking the policymakers they are trying to help for input. Without this input, the studies and analyses are less helpful in the decision-making process and give the appearance of policies being cherry picked for analysis.

> The truth is, the Trump tax cuts resulted in economic growth that was a full percentage point above CBO's forecast, and federal revenues far outpaced the agency's predictions. In fact, under Trump tax policies in 2022, tax revenues reached a record high of nearly $5 trillion, and revenues averaged $205 billion above CBO predictions for the four years following implementation of the law.

> Beyond what the Trump tax cuts did for economic growth and federal revenues, it provided major benefits to working families. The officially reported poverty level fell to its lowest rate in 50 years and unemployment rates for minorities and those without a college degree hit all-time lows. Real median household income rose by $5,000, and wages went up by nearly 5 percent. Americans earning under $100,000 saw an average tax cut of 16 percent. And while the tax burden on low-income families went down, the top one percent saw their share of federal taxes go up.[18]

Until 1981, the largest tax cuts in US history were the post-World War II era tax cuts initiated by President John F. Kennedy and enacted by President Lyndon Johnson in 1964. Once these tax cuts were signed into law, the economy expanded tremendously after suffering economic challenges in the years prior.

Then we had President Ronald Reagan's tax cuts early in his first term, followed by President George W. Bush's Tax cuts in 2001 and 2003, and the Trump tax cuts in 2017, all stimulated the US economy. Unfortunately, over time, Congresses and presidential administrations would alter the tax code by raising taxes and increasing government regulations, fueled by massive governmental spending on programs that were never funded properly. Every administration has stated they would be the one to roll back federal spending, but this never materialized.

The biggest problem Washington faces, and one we will detail in future chapters, is the broken nature of the federal government and the shortsightedness of our elected officials. Far too often, both political parties pass well-intentioned laws and programs, with disastrous results on the US economy. President Biden touted his domestic accomplishments, such as the American Rescue Plan. The Inflation Reduction Act, which incidentally had nothing to do with reducing inflation, was more of climate initiative — even Biden himself admitted this. One of his signature initiatives was the CHIPS Act. This science act was part of trillions of dollars worth of massive governmental spending, resulting in higher deficit spending. In all these policies, nothing went to small businesses across America. The only real beneficiary was corporate America. The CHIPS Act alone gave Intel Corporation over $18 billion to expand computer chip making in the US, only to have Intel layoff 15,000 workers — about 5 percent of its workforce.[19]

Intel is having difficulties in restructuring its chip-making operation, especially as it relates to national security, resulting in the US being dependent on overseas suppliers. With all the fanfare regarding the CHIPS Act, especially among Democrats, America needs to examine the role Intel plays with regard to America's national security. A November 2024 report for the Center for Strategic and International Studies highlights the importance of Intel.

While recent accounts of Intel's difficulties have mostly been confined to the business pages, the company's future has broad national and global significance far beyond its employees and shareholders. Intel is a critical player in the US government's efforts to reduce dependency on chips manufactured abroad—notably the significant concentration of production in Taiwan—and regain leadership in semiconductor manufacturing technology. Both capability and capacity are needed to provide an alternative source for the most advanced chips and a more resilient supply chain for foundational chips essential to the automotive, telecommunications, and medical sectors. If Intel's restructuring efforts fail, larger US efforts are unlikely to achieve their objectives, with significant ramifications for US national security and economic future. Indeed, as Geoff Colvin recently argued in Fortune, "Intel is no longer a conventional company and can no longer be evaluated as one . . . it's now a corporate actor on the geopolitical stage." Policymakers must recognize Intel's national security importance within this decade's dramatically changed geopolitical environment.[20]

As the fallout from the 2024 presidential election continues, many are still grappling with the fact that former President Donald Trump is back in the White House, and the Republican Party controls the House of Representatives and the US Senate. The Democrats and Democratic Candidate Vice President Kamala Harris focused on issues that were unrelated to the concerns of voters. The number one issue for voters was the economy, as former Democratic political strategist James Carvel coined in 1992, "It's the economy stupid." Democrats forgot this!

If America is to revive its economy, it will have to get serious about rebuilding US manufacturing, which both Democrats and Republicans have allowed to be outsourced to other countries. The COVID-19 pandemic placed to the forefront of Americans how failed policies of both Democrats and Republicans sent US manufacturing overseas, but most notably China.

Both Republicans and Democrats believed liberalizing trade with China would make them less authoritative and would move Beijing into the liberal economic order established by the United States after World War II. This proved false. All it did was hollow out US manufacturing, eliminating millions of jobs, and China became more authoritative, not less. During the COVID-19 pandemic,

many in this country were horrified to learn that products needed
to combat the pandemic, such as pharmaceuticals, were produced
in China. The problem about bringing back manufacturing to
the US is that many regions of the United States are considered a
manufacturing desert.

Both Democrats and Republicans have embraced free trade and
done everything they could to welcome China in the World Trade
Organization, all in the hope of embracing Beijing, in an effort to
become less authoritative. The strategy was for China to join the
liberal world order established by the United States. Instead, the
left-leaning Economic Policy Institute noted, all it did was create a
massive trade surplus in China's favor and destroy 3.7 million well-
paying US manufacturing jobs.[21]

Democratic and Republican administrations held to the belief
and passed legislation granting China free access to the American
market. Companies were allowed to outsource US manufacturing
to China, leading Beijing to be less authoritative. The net result was
the opposite: China was using the capital from the US to re-arm its
military and steal intellectual properties from US businesses, with no
repercussions from the US.

The other problem in bring in manufacturing back to the US,
is that companies don't set up manufacturing plants on the west
coast of the United States, especially in the most populous state in
the union. California is a horrible place to establish a business, let
alone a manufacturing plant. The regulatory burden, high taxes,
complex environmental laws, and anti-business labor rules stifle any
business startup. Even now, businesses are moving their corporate
headquarters to better business-friendly states such as Texas, Florida,
costal Carolinas, and the mid-west. The same is true for the anti-
business states of Oregon and Washington. The failed states of
Illinois, New York, and the New England states are considered toxic
for establishing a business.

These states believe in high governmental expenditures to fuel
their bloated government bureaucracy, coupled with massive
regulations and high taxes. Combined with a very hostile business
climate, businesses are prevented from trying to establish themselves.

America's Greatest National Security Threat

Billionaire business/investor Kevin O'Leary mentioned in February 2024, while speaking on Fox Business, that there are certain regions of the United States that you don't place a manufacturing plant. O'Leary has stated he is into establishing data centers for AI or artificial intelligence. Data centers are going to be scaled up in the coming years and you will need lots of energy to do this. Currently, data centers take up around 5 percent of all energy to run, in the next five years that will jump to 25 percent. Unfortunately, many regions of the US are unconsidered uninvestable because of their burdensome tax policies. Examples include California, Oregon, and Washington on the west coast, as well as Michigan, Illinois, New York, and the New England states in the east. The regulatory burdens, coupled with environmental laws, are so erroneous that you just don't set up businesses in these states.

Policies by Washington and the various states punish those workers who are part of the producer economy of manufacturing, logistics, and agriculture, with their push for a "Green New Deal" in the belief that wind and solar will eventually replace fossil fuel for America's energy needs. This is why President Trump campaigned on the notion that America needed to be energy independent, which means ending the Democrats' obsession with alternative energy as the primary source of the nation's energy security. Trump understood the needs and the concerns of the workers in industries heavily dependent on fossil fuels. These industries include construction, manufacturing, and agriculture—the very workers who make the nation's economy move forward.

> Trump does best with those industries, like construction, manufacturing, and agriculture, that actually make things. People who work with their hands—truck drivers, plumbers, electricians, oil-workers, and farmers—generally favour the Republicans and so do the people who employ them.[22]

The nation's political class often forgets about the working class. Washington and the political elites who work in tech, academia, and entertainment care very little about the blue-collar workers and do not hesitate to propose eliminating these sectors. What they fail to realize is that the working class keeps the US economy moving forward.

17

> Unlike those in the producer economy, tech, and other ephemeral industries tend to be less concerned about environmental regulations and labor laws; they rarely make anything in the United States and employ relatively few blue-collar or union workers.[23]

This push for a "Green New Deal" appeals to the academics and oligarch elites in the technological and government world but does not appeal to the working class — the ones the Democrats used to champion. California is a case study of rogue environmental policies which, in the pursuit of reducing greenhouse gas emissions, have quadrupled the cost of utilities for the working class. This created more unemployment among those working in the construction, manufacturing, agriculture, and logistic sectors.

Far too often there is a pervasive element in Washington, mainly among Democrats, that alternative energy will be this massive economic boom for the US economy and American workers. One example of this is the Biden administration's cancelation of the Keystone XL Pipeline, which resulted in the layoff of thousands of workers. Where are the new green jobs? When pressed, advocates for alternative energy reiterate their "we will produce millions of new green jobs" talking points. Reality has hit home as none of the words spoken by the Biden administration or Democrats in Washington and around the country have translated into reality.

Proponents of this new green conversion often mention that "fossil fuels are becoming obsolete and should be wiped out for the benefit of fitting a new economy." In spite of increased subsidies for wind and solar, fossil fuels "still represent roughly four-fifths of global energy generation, just as it did twenty years ago."

Germany is just one example of how the west is consumed with this push for alternative energy. The German government went all in on its own version of a new green deal by eliminating virtually its entire energy source in favor of alternative energy. As a result, the German economy contracted considerably, and now they can barely create enough energy to power their once vibrant manufacturing sector. Germany now has the highest cost for electricity in the European Union and have been mired in an economic recession for the past three years and now is heavily dependent on Russia for its energy needs. Because of their short-sightedness the US is supposed to expend our resources in protecting Germany from Russia but are unwilling to increase revenue for their own defense. Great Britain is an additional test case in which they have destroyed their economy in the pursuit of this elusive green energy. The evidence abounds that you can't generate enough energy solely with solar and wind to power a modern manufacturing-based economy. The only winner is China, the world's second-largest economy. China continues to flout the west's quest for alternative energy but "continues to open coal-fired plants a rapid rate."[24]

California is doing everything it can to eliminate fossil fuels in favor of alternative energy, such as solar and wind, for the states energy needs. For all of their efforts, all they have done is make the state dependent on other nations for its energy needs. Many are from Middle East countries, such as Saudia Arabia. California fails to understand that 6,000 products in our daily lives are made from oil derivatives that are manufactured out of crude oil.

The energy situation California faces is not just confined to the golden state, but to other states as well. Arizona receives about half its energy from California, and Nevada is 90 percent dependent on California for all its energy needs. Increases in energy prices in California means this state will feel the pain as well, plus other states across the country have been implementing California's draconian energy policies to the detriment of their states economic viability.

The California governor has lofty ambitions about running for president in 2028, and perusing his aspirational goals by buying into the new green philosophy. With his pursuit for higher office, Newsom is doing everything in his power to end the state's dependence on fossil fuels in favor of wind and solar. Everyone needs to understand all these sources are intermittent and only generate energy when the wind blows and the sun shines, but what about when they don't? For all of his lofty goals and for all of his virtue signaling, all he has done is drive the economic cost higher for the poor, the middle class, and business owners. This is why people and business are fleeing from the state to other areas of the US, notably Texas and Florida.[25]

With California's short-sightedness in its elusive "Green Agenda," the Air Resource Board approved a regulation with many expecting the state gasoline prices to spike forty-seven cents a gallon beginning next year. This may be fine for the wealthy, who drive Teslas and work from home or drive a short distance to work, but for millions of Californians who are forced to drive hours to work over crumbling roads, this extra cost just makes them poorer.

During the pandemic and all the recent natural disasters, we didn't need the tech oligarchs, government officials, the media, athletes, or entertainers, but we needed the construction workers, mechanics, first responders, truck drivers, and those working in the construction, manufacturing, agriculture, and logistics sectors.

> Recent US Supreme Court decision in *West Virginia v. Environmental Protection Agency* (2022), the justices held that agencies can't impose regulations dealing with major economic or policy questions unless Congress specifically authorizes them to do so. In *Loper Bright v. Raimondo* (2024), the court overturned the *Chevron* doctrine and held that federal courts should no longer defer to federal agencies' interpretations of the law or their own rulemaking authority. Together, these cases suggest that a plethora of current federal regulations exceed the authority Congress has granted under the law. [26]

These rulings returned the regulation of new laws back to the original constitutional intentions: enforcement is carried out by the executive branch and rule making is done by unelected bureaucrats in Washington.

The other difficulty in establishing a viable US manufacturing sector is the dismal state of America's educational system. The US spends over $800 billion a year on k-12 from federal, state, and local levels, per the US Census Bureau. More than half of all US children can't read at grade level. The US doesn't have enough skilled workers because we're not training people to be pipe fitters, electricians, welders, or other skilled craftsmen. In the following chapter, we will discuss how America's dismal educational system is a threat to America's national security.

An additional area, if used correctly, is the use of tariffs. Many have debated this topic on both sides of the political divide, but tariffs can be useful in forcing countries to negotiate fair trade, because free trade always hurts American companies. Far too often, our allies place tariffs on American products, but if the US reciprocates, we get blamed for instigating a trade war. Why is it that our allies can put tariffs on American products? Our allies in Europe subsidize Airbus. We don't do the same thing to Boeing. As soon as we institute fair trade and put tariffs on their products, they all complain,. Tariffs placed on American products hurt American workers by making American goods expensive and foreign products less expensive. China, for example, places tariffs on American products. Every US company that does business in China is forced to partner with a Chinese company and to turn over all intellectual property. This is not the case with Chinese companies, such as TikTok doing business in the US in 2024.

One of the big things President Trump is working on is US energy independence. We used to be energy independent. Now, we are energy dependent, even though we have the tools here. We pushed coal off to the side and began using natural gas. We dropped our greenhouse gases more so than Europe did, and Democrats still seem to have this idea that we can get all our energy from wind and solar. All that does is raise the cost of utilities. California has gone all-in on green energy, and their utility bills continue to rise. This harms the very people that they intend to help. We could sell liquid natural gas to Europe at fair market price that would wean them off Russian energy. The misguided EV mandate would only make us more dependent on China for energy needs, not less.

Two

The Civil Rights Issue of Our Times

T he greatest civil rights issue of our times is America's failing educational system! After the ending of the coronavirus, we've seen various national educational reports showing reading and math scores for American children in the K-12 system plummet. Half of all American kids cannot read or do math to grade level, this despite spending more than $850 billion from the federal, state, and local level annually on public K-12 education.[27]

The US has barely come to grips with America's dismal educational achievements in math and reading. The other catastrophic element in US education is the abysmal absenteeism rate among the nation's school children. It was bad before the onset of the coronavirus pandemic, which forced the closure of the nation's schools and suddenly skyrocketed the absenteeism rate to an astronomical high. Chronic absenteeism is defined as missing more than 10 percent of school days, or roughly eighteen days during the school year. Once schools were given permission to reopen, the absenteeism problem doubled nationally. The longer a student is absent from class over an extended period, the greater the likelihood that the child will fall further behind, and consequently will end up dropping out of school entirely.[28]

The nation must understand that if a child is not reading and doing math at or near grade level by fourth grade, the chances diminish significantly as the child further progresses in their academic life. Because of this, more and more children will drop out of school all together. This is a grave national security threat, because we are grooming the next generation of leaders.

For all the expenditures on education, prior to the coronavirus pandemic, American school children's reading and math scores were already beginning to drop. The Programme for International Student Assessment (PISA), is "an international assessment that measures what 15-year-old students have learned in math, reading and science." It is administered every three years to public and private school students in over sixty-four countries throughout the world. The latest PISA report had been postponed in 2021, but was given in 2022, so the next assessment will be given in 2025.

This international examination was created with input from thirty-seven industrial countries. These countries comprise the Organization for Economic Cooperation and Development (OECD). Back in 2018, before COVID-19 caused the lockdown of the nation schools, US students attending private and public schools took the exam and, just as in 2015, the results were not great. US students either improved slightly or regressed in both reading and mathematics. The results of the 2022 exams showed that American students improved in reading, but dramatically dropped in mathematics. Based on these results, America still ranks at the bottom of the list of industrialized countries.[29]

Other tests have produced similar results. In the fall of 2022, the National Assessment of Educational Progress (NAEP), often considered the nation's educational report card, released the first post-Covid testing results. They revealed a catastrophic regression in learning loss, with the sharpest reduction in math and reading for the nation's children in thirty years.[30]

Earlier this year, the same organization reported that children in fourth and eighth grades where the assessment was conducted tremendously regressed in both math and reading, despite billions spent on education during the pandemic. In addition to the lack of any meaningful progress in reading, the most dire failure is that US students are rapidly falling further behind. How many different educational initiatives have been put forth by both Democratic and Republican administrations? How many trillions of dollars have been spent over the decades to reach these dismal results?

> Fourth- and eighth-grade math scores saw the largest decline since the assessments were first administered in 1990. Average fourth-grade math scores declined five points, and average eighth-grade math scores declined eight points. Just one-third of eighth graders nationally are proficient in reading and math. Only 27 percent of eighth graders were proficient in math in 2022. Similarly, 31 percent of eighth graders scored proficient in reading in 2022.[31]

Other tests have produced similar results. Recent scores on The Trends in International Mathematics and Science Study (TIMSS), an assessment conducted by the National Center for Education Statistics (NCES), showed major drops in math and science.

> In math, the average US fourth- and eighth-grade scores were lower in 2023 than in 2019 (by 18 and 27 points, respectively). Math results for both grades are the lowest they have ever been since TIMSS began in 1995.

> In science, US scores have been declining since 2015, but compared to 2019, the 2023 declines were not statistically significant for either grade, according to NCES. Fourth-grade science test scores are the lowest they have ever been since 1995, and eighth-grade science scores are the same as they were in 1995.[32]

After spending trillions on education, the US has utterly failed to improve student achievement. Once again, American school children are faring far worse than their international competitors. Currently, American students barely master math and science concepts at grade level. This trend cannot continue! If America is to compete with other industrial countries and maintain national security, it is imperative for US students to be proficient in math and science. One of the greatest challenges America faces is competition from our adversaries in the latest technology such as Artificial Intelligence (AI). China is trying to take the lead and dominate this new technological innovation. The other area of global competition is found in the *next frontier* — space. American students must master space, but in order to do so, they must excel in both math and science.

With all the expenditures on education, shouldn't US student test scores be at least in the top five countries? Many would counter that additional resources need to be allocated, but there is no measurable calculation that more expenditures would improve educational outcomes. American students have made some improvements in key areas, but with the vast amount of spending on K-12, they should be doing far better than test scores show. We must understand that massive increases in school spending do not always equate to greater outcomes. Questions need to be asked. Who is accountable for how revenue from the Federal, State, and local government is being spent, considering the dismal test results? The US spends the most on education per pupil than any other industrial country, yet we have the worst outcomes; Why?

If America wants a vibrant and strong economy, it will need to re-shape and re-vamp its K-12 public school systems across the country. Far too many students are graduating without the necessary skills to compete in today's modern economy. In spite of America's dismal educational system being focused on Diversity, Equity, and Inclusion (DEI), the fact remains that minority students fare the worst, with over 70 percent of black and Hispanic students deficient at grade level in math and reading.[33]

As mentioned earlier, if a child is not reading at or near grade level by fourth grade, the chances of that child improving greatly diminishes, and more than likely results in the child dropping out of school before graduation. Individuals embedded in the education industrial complex voice continual rhetoric on how they care about America's children, but only seem to benefit from the educational misery these children face. They do nothing to fix America's educational disparity.

Former Republican candidate for President Vivek Ramaswamy ignited a firestorm when he posted on X, "Our American culture has venerated mediocrity over excellence for way too long (at least since the 90s and likely longer). That doesn't start in college, it starts YOUNG. A culture that celebrates the prom queen over the math Olympiad champ, or the jock over the valedictorian, will not produce the best engineers." He was correct. We could lambast him for his comments or we can fix America's dysfunctional educational system.

The US pours billions of dollars into Science, Technology, Engineering, and Math (STEM) education in elementary and high schools across the country. This is great news for the future, but what about the situation today? The US faces a shortage of individuals who are qualified to work in these fields—tech industries are struggling to find highly skilled, competent workers.

> In 2022, the United States Congress passed the CHIPS and Science Act, which aimed to increase national semiconductor manufacturing capacity and innovation. Amid concerns over the US's dwindling share of global chip-making, policymakers, and industry leaders were confronted with another challenge: a shortage of skilled technical workers, scientists, and engineers. Despite efforts to ramp up US STEM education capacity, including efforts to broaden the workforce pipeline by drawing in demographics historically underrepresented in these fields, the US remains highly reliant on foreign-born individuals for its high-tech workforce needs, particularly in the short term.[34]

> At the end of 2024, there was considerable debate over immigration regarding H-1B visas. First introduced in 1990, it is a temporary work permit for skilled workers. Many of the technology companies operating in Silicon Valley use the H-1B visas and hire non-citizens, instead of recruiting from local colleges and universities as they did in the past. According to a new report based on the 2016 US census data, around 71 percent of tech employees in the Silicon Valley and 50 percent in the San Francisco-Oakland-Hayward region are not born in the US.[35]

What needs to be addressed about what many who support H-1B is the weaknesses of the US educational system. The nation's education system did not prepare today's young adults for the jobs that are needed today. Instead, the focus is on minuscule or "woke" progressive majors and studies. Recently, the US has been pouring billions of dollars into Science, Technology, Engineering, and Math (STEM) education in elementary and high schools across the country. This is great for the future, but what about the situation today? The US faces a shortage of individuals who are qualified to work in these fields—tech industries are struggling to find highly skilled, competent workers.

While training and educating STEM talent domestically among elementary school and high school students will address future workforce needs, it is more of a generational strategy—one that does not solve the acute, near-term shortages that high-tech industries and US federal S&E-related agencies struggle with. According to the Semiconductor Industry Association, the US economy is projected to have approximately 1.4 million unfilled computer science, engineering, and technician jobs by 2030. Given the national security and economic advantages of US leadership in science and engineering, US policies must ensure that the US remains an attractive destination for foreign STEM talent and that non-citizen foreign-born S&E professionals can remain in the US after graduation. [36]

One of the greatest national security threats the US faces is China's higher education system, which graduates six times as many students with bachelor's degrees in engineering and computer science than colleges in the US. Engineering majors comprise 33 percent of China's college students, but only 5 percent of America's scholars are majoring in engineering. China also leads with STEM subject graduates, numbering 4.7 million as opposed to only 568,000 in the US. These are sobering statistics. America needs to wake up!

Major company CEOs recognized this years ago and took their business elsewhere. Tim Cook, the late former Apple CEO, put the numbers into perspective. He rationalized his production locations in the Middle Kingdom with a visual explanation. "In the US, you could have a meeting of tooling engineers, and I'm not sure we could fill the room. In China, you could fill multiple football fields."

Higher education is not alone in failing the US job market. Elon Musk stated, "Colleges are basically for fun and to prove you can do your chores, but they're not for learning." Trade schools are a necessary component in preparing students for practical careers. Unfortunately, while trade schools in other countries excel in filling "average" jobs with enthusiastic, skilled individuals, there is a severe shortage of such workers in the United States.

In fact, the biggest skills gap is not at the top of the job pyramid, as techies insist, but further down. The success of countries like Japan, for example, rests with 'superior averageness' that leverages the efforts of workers on the factory floor. In the US, the big shortfall will not be among college grads, but at the production level. A key reason is the US's traditionally weak trade-school education. It's hard to build factories, particularly using the latest technology, with an ageing workforce. Right now, estimates suggest as many as 600,000 new manufacturing jobs generated this decade won't be filled. And there is no deep bench of talent waiting to replace retirees. Fifty percent of the active workers in manufacturing are above the age of 45. The current shortage of welders, now 240,000, could grow to 360,000 by 2027.[37]

Too many in the educational and political establishments are firmly embedded into the educational-industrial complex, believing we just need to spend more on education, but is that really the answer? According to the US Census Bureau's Annual Survey of School System Finances Data, "Average US public school spending per pupil in elementary and secondary schools rose 8.9% to $15,633 in fiscal year (FY) 2022 from the previous year."

The Census Bureau's report identified the states with the highest and lowest spending per pupil. Topping the list were the highest spenders: New York ($29,873), District of Columbia ($27,425), New Jersey ($25,099), Vermont ($24,453), and Connecticut ($24,453).

States with the lowest per pupil spending were Utah ($9,552), Idaho ($9,670), Arizona ($10,315), Oklahoma ($10,890), and Mississippi ($10,984). All nine states in the Northeast region ranked in the top fourteen for current per pupil spending, and seven were in the top ten.

Sixteen of the twenty states with the lowest per pupil spending were in the South or West. Iowa, Missouri, Indiana, and South Dakota were the remaining four states.

Among the nation's one hundred largest school systems by enrollment, the New York City School District in New York ($35,914) spent the most per pupil in FY 2022, followed by Washington Schools in the District of Columbia ($27,425); San Francisco Unified in California ($23,654); Atlanta School District in Georgia ($22,882); Los Angeles Unified in California ($21,940); and Detroit School District in Michigan ($21,771).[38]

Two of the largest and highest-spending school districts — New York City School District ($38.5 billion) and Los Angeles Unified ($12.5 billion), received the most funding from federal, state, and local sources. At the same time, both districts have disastrous test results and a high educational achievement gap for their students, especially among black and Hispanic students.[39]

Why is it that the states and cities with the greatest spending on education have the most educational achievement disparity? Just examine a report from The Office of the New York State Comptroller, which focused on fourth-grade math scores.

> Proficiency rates declined 8 percentage points from 2019 for White students, 6 points for Hispanic students and 3 points for Black students. Declines were steepest for Asian and Pacific Islander fourth graders, for whom math proficiency declined 14 percentage points. In 2022, proficiency rates were 55 percent for Asian students, [39] percent for White students, 15 percent for Hispanic students, and 14 percent for Black students. From 2019 to 2022, achievement gaps in proficiency rates between White students and Black or Hispanic students in New York generally remained steady or even closed slightly.[40]

With all of New York's spending and prominently touted efforts on diversity, equity, and inclusion (DEI), why is there such a dismal educational achievement gap, especially for minority students? Each year, the gap grows wider and wider, further cementing these children to a life of economic hardship. Where is the accountability for all this spending?

The Los Angeles Unified School System is all in on massive spending for education, but they too have one of the worst outcomes for educational results. The past two years have shown a slight increase in state test scores, but they are still well below pre-COVID-19 levels. Again, where is the accountability?[41]

Examine other schools across the country, beginning with Baltimore, The Maryland Department of Education released a report that should outrage anyone who cares about public education! The report showed that twenty-three schools, including elementary, middle, and high schools in the city of Baltimore had zero students who tested proficient in math. Not a single student! Astoundingly, two thousand students who took the state test could not do math at grade level!

What was not added in the report was an additional twenty schools that each had only one student who could pass the math proficiency at grade level. Even in the five "elite" high schools, only 11.4 percent could do math at grade level.

Digging deeper into the report, 41 percent of students in the Baltimore system have a 1.0 (D) GPA or less. In the Baltimore city school district, 75 percent of the students are black.[42]

Rather than address this disastrous educational achievement, the schools just wave the graduation requirements and graduate the students. What kind of economic opportunities await them when they are only doing math and reading at a middle school level?

If this wasn't bad enough, in 2022, Baltimore Superintendent of Public Education Dr. Sonja Santelises received a raise with a total compensation package of over $444,000, What was the metric for this considering the deplorable educational results standards for the city's children, with the vast amount impacting children of color? What metric was used for Santelises receiving a raise? Where was the state of Maryland in educational oversight, as this couldn't have been a singular aberration, but something that was years in the making. The superintendent's numerous awards and even her own words do not reflect a district with such dismal achievements.

> Dr. Santelises is a two-time finalist for the Council of the Great City Schools' Urban Educator of the Year, its highest honor for superintendents across the country. She was first honored in 2020, and again in October 2024. Also, she was a 2023 honoree as one of Maryland's Most Admired CEOs by The Daily Record.

> "My desire, focus, and drive remain to ensure every Baltimore City student graduates prepared for higher education and a family-sustaining career. Much has been accomplished during the last eight years, but more successes are ahead. I am pleased that the Board shares my desire to see that work through," said Dr. Santelises. "All along, I have been focused on doing what is right for children and families."[43]

When this report was released, we heard nothing from all the leaders who claim to care about children of color, considering 80 percent of Baltimore Public School children are black! So, where are Black Lives Matter, all the civil rights leaders, the professional athletes, the Democratic elected representatives, and Presidents Biden, Clinton, and Obama?

Where is the National Association for the Advancement of Colored People (NAACP), who incidentally is headquartered in Baltimore? Do the leaders get out and see the misery for children of color in the city schools? And for that matter, what is transpiring across the country for black and Hispanic children?

Where is President Obama on this subject, especially as it impacts black children? One only has to remember when he was an obscure State Senator from Illinois, and he gave the Keynote address at the Democratic National Convention in 2004, "If there's a child on the south side of Chicago who can't read, that matters to me, even if it's not my child."

I guess he doesn't care, because he is part of the educational-industrial complex, except his children were able to opt out of the public school system all together by attending a prestigious private school in the Washington, DC area. His children have never attended public school, as they have attended private schools their entire childhood. President Obama was against school choice for families who want to opt their children out for the failing DC school system, but he had choice for his children.

One of President Obama's first official acts as president was to end a very successful DC school voucher program that enabled students to receive vouchers to attend private schools, including the very school Obama's daughter were able to attend. Obama canceled this program, and these children were sent back to the failing DC public school system.

Even liberal columnist Juan Williams criticized this move by Obama.

> The cause of my upset is watching the key civil rights issue of this generation—improving big city public school education—get tossed overboard by political gamesmanship . . . If there is one goal that deserves to be held above day-to-day partisanship and pettiness of ordinary politics it is the effort to end the scandalous poor level of academic achievement and abysmally high drop-out rates for America's black and Hispanic students . . . With no living, breathing students profiting from the program to give it a face and stand and defend it the Congress has little political pressure to put new money into the program. The political pressure will be coming exclusively from the teacher's unions who oppose the vouchers, just as they oppose No Child Left Behind and charter schools and every other effort at reforming public

schools that continue to fail the nation's most vulnerable young people, low-income blacks and Hispanics . . . The National Education Association and other teachers' unions have put millions into Democrats' congressional campaigns because they oppose Republican efforts to challenge unions on their resistance to school reform and specifically their refusal to support ideas such as performance-based pay for teachers who raise students' test scores.[44]

Elected leaders will always point out that what the nation needs to do is allocate more resources to public schools, but many of the top spending public school districts in the country have the worst performing school districts. New York topped the per capita spending at $29,000 per child, with the nation's capital of Washington, DC. at close to $27,000. The city of Baltimore placed in the top three for per pupil spending at close to $22,000 and this is the results they get.

The state of Illinois is also experiencing educational disparity. Test data from 2023 indicates that students attending Chicago's Public Schools are at just as much of a disadvantage as their peers in other cities. This is especially true for low-income, Black, and Hispanic students.

Just 19 percent of third through eighth-grade students from low-income families met proficiency standards in reading and 11 percent in math . . . just 14 percent of low-income eleventh-grade students met reading proficiency and 12 percent met math goals on the Standardized Achievement Test used for college admissions. The proficiency rate for low-income high school students on the SAT was eight percentage points lower than the districtwide in reading and seven percentage points lower in math.[45]

The rest of Illinois follows the same pattern as Chicago. *Wirepoints* issued a stinging report condemning the entire Illinois educational system on how it educates the state's children.

Wirepoints is an independent, nonprofit company delivering original research and commentary about Illinois' economy and government, who has a particular focus on the Illinois state and local fiscal crises. We try to stick to policy, facts, and numbers, not politics.

Inside the report it highlighted the fact that in Decatur's public-school third-graders in 2019, just 2 percent of black and 16 percent of white students could read at grade level. In Rockford, it was 7 percent of black students. In the state capital of Peoria, 8 percent of blacks. And in Elgin, just 11 percent of Hispanic third-graders could read at grade level. Similar results can be found across the state.[46]

Just examine Oregon, which eliminated any testing requirements to graduate high school because it disproportionally impacts children of color. Instead of addressing this educational disparity, the answer is to remove the testing standards all together. How does this help black and Hispanic children?

This was supposed to be temporary, but Oregon extended the policy another five years. Instead of giving these students a level of educational proficiency, where they will be able to excel in a modern economy, they are now sent out into the world where many will be dependent on the government or end up in prison because of a lack of core educational competence.

The same dismal educational results can be found across the country, even in Washington, DC.

Prior to the pandemic, the DC public school system had a dismal educational achievement gap, where 70 percent of students were unable to do math and English to grade level. This was further amplified by the forced government lockdown of the nation's schools.

The first post-pandemic student assessment showed a massive drop in math and reading.

> While reading proficiency dropped by roughly 5% for white students from 2019 to 2022, proficiency for Hispanic Latino students fell by 7%, and 7.7% for Black students. In math, proficiency rates dropped by 12% for Black students and 13% for Hispanic Latino students, compared to 8.7% for white students. [47]

Early in 2022, the Washington Post reported proficiency rates showing a similar achievement gap.

> Twenty-eight percent of Black students and 30 percent of Hispanic students were considered proficient on a test administered in fall 2021, according to the data. Seventy percent of White students hit these benchmarks. In fall 2019, 44 percent of Black students and 42 percent of Hispanic students hit these benchmarks, compared with 73 percent of White students. [48]

Where is the accountability for these children?

The National Center for Educational Statistics reported that Washington, DC spends on average just shy of $30,000 per student, but with all this revenue why then does the DC school system have such a dismal educational achievement especially for the 70% of its black students?[49]

You would think there would be accountability, but the teachers and educational bureaucracy enjoy some of the most lucrative benefits albeit supported by their union benefactors. Where is the accountability for the children of Illinois?

The deteriorating nature of US public education has awakened a parental tsunami. First, it was from the forced Covid lockdowns, then it was the dismal educational standards then the *woke* atmosphere pushed on American children. Schools have forced parents to abandon public schools in droves for various alternative schooling.

All throughout the country, attendance at the nation's public schools is down considerably as parents are making the decision to either home-school their children or place them in religious-themed schools, which are up 35 percent from 2019.

Unfortunately, the Democratic Party is failing to understand this monumental tsunami as parents want more school choice, not less! Republicans seem to have gotten the message. Republican governors across the country are signing legislation giving parents more education options on where, how, and what their children learn.

One only must look no further than the gubernatorial election in Virginia, where in 2021, the Republican candidate used options for education as the central theme of his candidacy. His Democratic opponent was against school choice and uttered the famous phrase "I don't think parents should be telling schools what they should teach." This enraged parents, and the Republican Gubernatorial candidate Glenn Youngkin rode to victory in a state that hadn't elected a Republican in over ten years.

So far, Republicans have heard the siren call from parents as various GOP governors have enacted sweeping school choice reforms in their various states. Unfortunately, Democrats are still shackled against the principle of any school choice.

The main impetus for the Democrats in rejecting school choice is that they are intertwined at the hip with the powerful teachers unions. These unions are adamantly opposed to any school choice, and incidentally, give millions exclusively to the Democratic Party.

All throughout the coronavirus pandemic, the teachers unions worked with Democrats in keeping schools closed. No matter that the science stated that children are not impacted by the viruses spread and no other country kept schools closed for as long as the US did. The forced school closure had a devastating impact on the mental and scholastic ability of the nation's children.

Just examine the salary of Randi Weingarten of the American Federation of Teachers (AFT). The second-largest national teacher's union in the United States has a salary of over $500,000 and was instrumental in working with the Centers for Disease Control in extending the lockdown for the nation's school-age children. Rebecca S. Pringle, the President of the National Education Association (NEA), the largest teacher's union, has a similar base salary, with both Weingarten and Pringle strong proponents against school choice. Total contributions of teacher's union political donations to Democrats totaled just shy of $45 million.

It's ironic that Democrats are totally against school choice but at the same time opt their own children out of public education for private schools. Presidents Carter, Clinton, Obama, and Biden all sent their own children to private schools, but have done everything they could to keep parents from having the same choice.

The Governor of California, Gavin Newsom, kept six million Californian children in K-12 locked out and learning on Zoom. Yet, he opted his own children out of public school and placed them in a $60,000 a year private school in the exclusive wealthy enclave on Ross, located in Marin County, one of the wealthiest counties in the US.

Maybe the reason for animus against school choice for the nation's children is that it means fewer donations flowing to political coffers who only want to keep the status quo. America desperately needs a major overhaul of its entire educational system, beginning with the nation's K-12 schools. The focus needs to be on preparing American students for post-secondary education, which includes college and universities as well as trade and vocational education.

For far too long, American education has disinvested in vocational and trade education in high schools by preparing all students for post-secondary schooling in colleges and universities. For some reason, our political leaders have placed an emphasis on college, insisting that if you haven't graduated from a college or university, you are not as smart as someone who did. The entire 2024 presidential election was predicated on blue-collar workers across America thumbing their nose at the elites. The educated elites of both political parties stated that inflation was temporary or transitory, but it's now permanent! Inflation placed the nation's finances in a precarious situation, with $36 trillion in debt.

One only has to remember the past few years. During the pandemic and the various natural disasters, we didn't need the politician, the Wall Street banker, the entertainer, or athlete. We needed the first responder, the mechanic, the utility lineman, the truck driver and every other blue-collar job that kept the US economy humming while the rest of the nation was shut down.

If America is to revitalize its manufacturing industrial base, we need to bring back technical and trade schools such as welders, pipefitters, electricians, and other building trades. With the US in global competition with Europe, Japan, and especially China, America needs to focus on technical trades such as technology or high tech. Technological trades are predicated on cyber security, drones, and other high-technological training, beginning in the high school and then transferring to technical training schools, where certifications can be obtained, preparing students for employment in the twenty-first century economy.

In our K-12 school system, emphasis does not need to be placed on woke ideology that indoctrinates students to think a particular way. Instead of teaching students to pass standardized tests or encouraging children to follow popular trends, Finland's teachers are focused on helping students to develop critical thinking skills and increase media literacy. Beginning with pre-school and continuing throughout every grade level in all subjects, this extraordinary teaching and learning process consistently produces unparalleled results.

Teaching is a prestigious profession in Finland. Unlike most of their American counterparts, Finland's teachers are given leeway to refine and master the art of teaching. They are able to create and adapt unique learning opportunities for students without facing the pressures of high-stakes testing and teacher evaluations.[50]

By recalibrating K-12 on practical education by having learn concepts and not on standardized testing. US students need to focus on courses in science, mathematics, and other core subjects, plus end the woke educational curriculum. Constitutional Law Professor Jonathan Turley at George Washington University wrote a book, *The Indispensable Right: Free Speech in an Age of Rage*, in which he discusses many of these principles that are now prevalent in K-12 and colleges/universities across the country. If education also emphasized trade and technical trade schools, it would empower many students to pursue other career paths, as many who do not want the college experience or want to obtain other opportunities would not be saddled with massive student loan debt crisis faced by graduating students.

The US Supreme Court overturned President Biden's attempt to forgive student loans, as a president doesn't have the authority under the constitution to unilaterally cancel student loan debt. This is in the prevue of Congress, where it states, "No Money shall be drawn from the Treasury, but in Consequence of Appropriations made by Law." This is what is precisely stated in Section one Article eight of the US Constitution.

What has not been reported is that the student loan debt was a problem in 2010, but the Democrats, led by President Obama and Vice President Biden, decided to nationalize the student loan program instead of having it administrated by financial institutions. In 2010, Obama and the Democratic Party made it dramatically worse, with the passage of the Health Care and Education Reconciliation Act; a little-known rider was added called the Student Aid and Fiscal Responsibility Act, which fundamentally changed the way student loans were granted.

A rider is an additional provision that is added to a bill or other measure under consideration by Congress that has nothing to do with the subject matter of the main bill. In this case, the rider was attached to Obamacare.

The healthcare reform bill was passed and signed into law by President Obama on a strictly partisan vote with not one Republican voting in favor. Like healthcare, the Student Aid and Fiscal Responsibility Act had an extreme adverse effect. Instead of making college and university less expensive, it exploded the cost, and with it, student loan debt quadrupled tenfold.

Prior to the passage of this game-changing legislation signed into law by President Obama, student loans were issued as guaranteed loans, with the banks as the loan agent and the terms determined by the federal government. After its passage, the federal government assumed all responsibilities for student loans and the banks were eliminated from the entire process.

Unfortunately, this had the opposite effect, as college and universities raised the cost of tuition. The institutions were aware that students wanted a college education, and the federal government would back all student loans. The act did nothing to rein in college spending. Instead, the non-academic side of higher education, namely the administrative bureaucracy, exploded far faster than any other cost.

Biden did nothing to address the root cause of higher college costs. He directed the financial burden to the US taxpayers, and the many who paid off their student loan or never attended college.

Numerous educational achievement results have shown that three-quarters of eighth graders are not proficient in math, while 69 percent are not meeting reading proficiency. Just think about this for a minute—only one in four American kids are proficient at grade level in math, with few obtaining any kind of proficiency in advanced mathematics. Does anyone wonder why few high school graduates are prepared for introductory college classes?

How is America supposed to compete with the rest of the world, especially our number one competitor China? America has faced challenges before. In 1957, Russia launched Sputnik, a Soviet satellite, which challenged America's perceived educational deficiencies. Within a year, the US invested heavily in high-quality educational learning in science, mathematics, and foreign languages. This singular moment awakened America and prompted our political system to re-examine US education.

America's failed educational system, if not reformed, will threaten the national security of the country. What we have right now is a Sputnik-like moment. How the United States responds will determine the future for our children!

Three

America's Dysfunctional Political System

I f America is to have a viable and robust foreign policy, it will have to address the extreme dysfunction in its political system. The nation just endured its most partisan election in the postmodern era where each side demonized the other in the most despicable manner. When the Democratic and Republican parties do gain power, they only appeal to their respective base instead of reaching consensus with the other side.

> America's political system is now fractured, disputatious, and dispiriting. Both dominant political parties have adopted the same strategy to win elections— mobilize their angry base voters and exploit real or invented flaws in the opponent to sway unaffiliated voters. Fear and anger are seen as more powerful motivating sentiments to win elections than are specific proposals or broad sentiments of hope and encouragement. This rancorous politics projects grotesque images on the international stage, images exploited by opponents and occasionally by friends. It is hard to see how America can continue to be a welcome leader in the world when it is riven by bitter politics at home.[51]

In the past decade, almost all consequential legislation passed was done in a partisan manner, without input from the other political party. Each side blamed the other for the partisanship found in Washington. The 2024 presidential election, if you examine it differently from the political elites, was that the American people want their elected officials to work on improving the economy, fixing our broken immigration system, and ending the open border policies of the Biden administration, making our communities safer. The key takeaway is to improve the lives of the American people.

If you take a page from history, President Ronald Reagan was able to reach across the political aisle and work with Democrats in passing much of his economic agenda. He was famously quoted when speaking to his Chief of Staff James Baker: "I'd rather get 80 percent of what I want than go over the cliff with my flags flying." In 1986, he was able to pass his signature Tax Reform legislation while working with then Democratic Speaker of the House Thomas Phillip "Tip" O'Neill Jr of Massachusetts. At the conclusion of the landmark tax reform legislation, O'Neill mentioned to his base that we just raised taxes, with Reagan stating we just cut taxes. Neither was willing to criticize the other, as they knew they had to give something to their respective base of their party. Today, neither party can seem to work with the other side. They have turned it into a zero-sum game where winning is more important than working in a bipartisan manner to solve the nation's most pressing problems.

Far too often, both Congress and the executive branch have abdicated their constitutional duties regarding the budget and have relied on continuing resolutions to fund the government. Over the years, they have used continuing resolutions as the main avenue in passing a budget. This process has been one adjunct failure! It only brings the nation to the brink of fiscal catastrophe. This process of continuing resolutions to properly fund the government fails in every way and only leads to a national security crisis.

The political division the nation is going through also factors into one of the core responsibilities of the federal government — to pass a yearly budget on time. In the past decades, each administration failed to pass an annual budget. In the absence of a budget, the nation just passes a continuing resolution that kicks the can down the road a few months or later. Both the Congress and President blame each other for the stalemate, and that pushes the country into a fiscal crisis. Just before the country reaches the abyss, they vote on another continuing resolution, and the process starts again. Even now, the country is operating off a continuing resolution which will only be extended by another continuing resolution.

A continuing resolution (CR) can serve a temporary purpose by avoiding a government shutdown that both sides do not want, but it should be used sparingly. In the not-too-distant past, all appropriations bills went through their respective committees to debate the merits of increases or reductions, then voted on by committee before being accepted or rejected by the House of Representatives and Senate, compromises would be made before final passage and then signed by the president. That was in the past. Now, we literally have open warfare where both sides look at as a zero-sum game and only want to embrace and defeat the other sides. The real loser in the entire process is the American people.

Instead of the constitutionally mandated manner of passing the twelve appropriations bills, the nation's elected officials utilize continuing resolutions to fund the US government. In the past, this method was rarely used, but in the twenty-first century, this budgetary process has been used well over 136 times. Each year, the continuing resolutions last longer and are more disruptive to properly fund the government. Again, during this century alone, continuing resolutions funded the government for a few months. Some lasted a half a year, and numerous times, continuing resolutions funded the government for the entire year, causing major disruptions to agencies' budgets.[52]

The continual use of utilizing continuing resolutions to fund the government has serious potential to disrupt and threaten US national security. In 2024, the Center for Strategic and International Studies outlined the impact of CRs on defense programs:

> Given the frequency with which the Pentagon begins the fiscal year under a stopgap funding extension, short-term CRs of 2-3 months may not cause major disruptions to the execution of defense programs. However, longer CRs that extend into the new calendar year can significantly disrupt programs that are forced to operate with spending levels lower than or higher than what they had projected. Moreover, the military services cannot fund "new start" programs or increase production rates under a

CR. In a letter to congressional appropriators, Secretary of the Air Force Frank Kendall outlined that the -6month CR originally proposed by Speaker Johnson would prevent production increases for munitions stockpiles and reduce aircraft mission capable rates. Once regular appropriations have been passed after a long-term CR, DOD programs still face "serious execution problems," as they have limited time to negotiate contracts and efficiently spend operating funds before they expire at the end of the fiscal year on September 30.[53]

Both the Congress and the executive branch need to get back to a bygone time when the president submits a budget to the Congress and the resident committees debate the twelve appropriation bills. Both sides have witnesses and experts debate the merits of each appropriation. This may be naïve on my part, but it was the way it has been done in the past, and both parties must realize you do not get everything you want.

One major legislative tool Congress uses and must end is earmarks. Members can insert earmarks into any of the discretionary appropriation bills, directing funding to a specific member's spending priority in their district or state. This circumvents the process and adds billions to the specific appropriation. Each legislative decision should be a stand-alone, which only deals with the matter at hand.

Another significant problem facing the dysfunctional political system is the way the three branches of government have lost sight of their constitutional responsibilities, encapsulated in the US Constitution. Over the decades, we have witnessed and accepted Congress delegating much of its core legislative responsibility to the executive branch. Far too long, Congress has allowed and accepted executive overreach into its core constitutional responsibilities. A couple of those key areas is budgeting, namely President Biden's push to unilaterally forgive student loan debt. Many have estimated this to cost between $500 billion to upwards of a trillion dollars. The US Supreme Court rejected this policy as a clear usurpation of Congress, namely that all revenues originate in the House of Representatives not by fiat by any president now and into the future.

The US Constitution is clear on this matter as written in Article One Section Two, "The Congress shall have Power To lay and collect

Taxes, Duties, Imposts, and Excises, to pay the Debts and provide for the common Defense and general Welfare of the United States; but all Duties, Imposts, and Excises shall be uniform throughout the United States." The president doesn't have this power.

President Biden was using the Higher Education Relief Opportunities for Students (HEROES) Act of 2003. This was a loan forgiveness program but was specifically intended to assist military personnel deployed to combat zones in support of the wars in Iraq and Afghanistan.

Even then Speaker of the House of Representatives Nancy Pelosi (D-Calif.) stated, "People think that the President of the United States has the power for debt forgiveness. He does not. He can postpone. He can delay. But he does not have that power. That has to be an act of Congress."

Speaking before the House of Representatives Committee on Judiciary on May 15, 2019, Constitutional Law Professor at George Washington University Jonathan Turley stated:

> My prior testimony before both the Senate and the House of Representatives has warned of increasing executive encroachment on legislative authority and asserted the need for Congress to be more aggressive in defending its Article I authority—particularly in its appropriation and oversight functions. Indeed, I have served as legal counsel for members of this body— including the House of Representatives as a whole—in defending its inherent powers from executive overreach and excess. With the shifting fortunes of politics, the commitment to the separation of powers tends to wane with control of the White House, as discussed below. Yet, I hope that all members of this Committee share the institutional interest in protecting existing precedent on congressional authority and jurisdiction.[54]

Before Speaking before the Judiciary Committee, Turley spoke before the House Committee on the Judiciary Subcommittee on The Constitution, Civil Rights, and Civil Liberties.

> I have repeatedly testified before both the House and the Senate to implore members to reclaim their inherent powers and exercise legislative authority in our government. Instead, members have frittered away their Article I powers to an ever-expanding executive branch . . . At the same time, Congress has continued (despite objections by some of us) to appropriate

billions of dollars to the Executive Branch with few conditions attached. The current controversy is the result of this long and irresponsible history.[55]

The crisis at the US southern border is a direct result of Congress failing to do its constitutional responsibility by allocating billions to the executive branch without oversite. Immigration is where Congress has allowed the executive branch to issue executive orders on all immigration-related matters. Both political parties will blame each other for failing to pass comprehensive immigration reform — even the latest attempt that was tried in 2024 was unfairly blamed on former President Donald Trump. If one had just examined the entirety of the bill, it really did nothing to stop the flow of illegal immigrants into the country. It was more of a partisan attempt at immigration reform measure in name only. Inside the bill it still allows 5,000 illegals to cross into the US every day, does nothing about amnesty for illegal immigrants who enter the country.

Former Homeland Security Director during the Obama administration, Jeh Johnson, discussed border security in 2019 on MSNBC's *Morning Joe*.

> When I was in office at former Secretary of Homeland Security Kirsten Nielsen's job, at her desk, I'd get to work around 6:30 in the morning and there'd be my intelligence book, sitting on my desk . . . The PDB and also the apprehension numbers from the day before. And I'd look at them every morning — and my staff will tell you if it was under 1,000 apprehensions the day before that was a relatively good number. And if it was above 1,000 that was a relatively bad number, and I was going to be in a bad mood the whole day . . . On Tuesday there were 4,000 apprehensions. I know that a thousand overwhelms the system. I cannot begin to imagine what 4,000 a day looks like, so we are truly in a crisis.[56]

Congress has again failed in its constitutional duties by passing ambiguous legislation and thus allowing the executive agencies to interpret the laws as they see fit. In essence, you have unelected federal bureaucrats usurping the constitutional responsibilities encapsulated in the US constitution to others. This way, Congress can wash their hands of any responsibilities or culpability in the laws they pass. Even the states have jumped on this trend, especially California where they are forcing other states and the nation to accept their standards on a host of regulations. Even though interstate commerce is the sole arbitrator of the federal government per various US Supreme Court decisions and the US constitution.

> Two recent US Supreme Court decisions have reversed overreach by federal agencies and lack of Congressional legislation in both in *West Virginia v. Environmental Protection Agency* (2022), the justices held that agencies can't impose regulations dealing with major economic or policy questions unless Congress specifically authorizes them to do so. In *Loper Bright v. Raimondo* (2024), the court overturned the *Chevron* doctrine and held that federal courts should no longer defer to federal agencies' interpretations of the law or their own rulemaking authority. Together, these cases suggest that a plethora of current federal regulations exceed the authority Congress has granted under the law.[57]

Democrats are appalled with these rulings. Over the course of the past few years, they have attacked the integrity and independence of the US Supreme Court, especially in light of the decision in *Dobbs v. Jackson Women's Health Organization,* which held the Constitution doesn't confer the right to an abortion. The US Supreme Court sent the decision on abortion to be debated at the state level.

Throughout President Biden's term in office, Democrats argued for the need for radical change as it relates to the US Supreme Court, and in June 2024, the president held a Zoom call with the Congressional Progressive Caucus, chaired by Rep. Pramila Jayapal (D.-Wash.) and co-chaired by Rep. Ilhan Omar (D-Minn.). The primary focus of the Zoom meeting was how to radically alter the makeup of the US Supreme Court.

Various liberal professors, political pundits, and political officials have attacked the US Supreme Court. In her claim to uphold the constitution, Liberal Sen. Elizabeth Warren (D-Mass.), has demanded that the court be packed with justices. What she was angling for was the court to rule in her favor.

The argument about recalibrating the US Supreme Court is not for the benefit of the American people, but a direct assault on the past rulings they disagree with. The proposal is really a direct assault on the US Supreme Court and a way to change its makeup through "court packing, court purging, ending life tenure, 'ethics' codes and a host of other troubling proposals."[58]

An independent judiciary has always been the hallmark of the US constitutional Republic ever since Chief Justice John Marshall handed down his pivotal and legendary US Supreme Court ruling in the landmark case of Marbury v. Madison.

Chief Justice John Marshall's 34-year tenure as the father of the US Supreme Court spanned six presidential administrations. By his judicial acumen, he established the court as a co-equal branch of government alongside the legislative and executive branches of government. Many precedents established by Marshall are the very foundations of American constitutional law that continue to be upheld to this very day. The very ability of the US Supreme Court to interpret the constitutionality of legislation and executive actions is still as important today as it was in the past. An independent judiciary is the hallmark of our constitutional republic and would be forever altered if changed purely for partisan purposes. This co-equal branch has been one of the pivotal aspects of America's constitutional Republic by having an independent judiciary.[59]

Alexander Hamilton, writing in Federalist #78 stated the importance of an independent judiciary in keeping the other two branches of government, namely the legislative and executive branch, adhering to the principles set forth in the constitution.

> Whoever attentively considers the different departments of power must perceive, that, in a government in which they are separated from each other, the judiciary, from the nature of its functions, will always be the least dangerous to the political rights of the Constitution; because it will be least in a capacity to annoy or injure them. The Executive not only dispenses the honors but holds the sword of the community. The legislature not only commands the purse but prescribes the rules by which the duties and rights of every citizen are to be regulated. The judiciary, on the contrary, has no influence over either the sword or the purse; no direction either of the strength or of the wealth of the society; and can take no active resolution whatever. It may truly be said to have neither FORCE nor WILL, but merely judgment; and must ultimately depend upon the aid of the executive arm even for the efficacy of its judgments.
>
> This simple view of the matter suggests several important consequences. It

proves incontestably, that the judiciary is beyond comparison the weakest of the three departments of power; that it can never attack with success either of the other two; and that all possible care is requisite to enable it to defend itself against their attacks. It equally proves, that though individual oppression may now and then proceed from the courts of justice, the general liberty of the people can never be endangered from that quarter; I mean so long as the judiciary remains truly distinct from both the legislature and the Executive. For I agree, that "there is no liberty, if the power of judging be not separated from the legislative and executive powers." And it proves, in the last place, that as liberty can have nothing to fear from the judiciary alone, but would have everything to fear from its union with either of the other departments; that as all the effects of such a union must ensue from a dependence of the former on the latter, notwithstanding a nominal and apparent separation; that as, from the natural feebleness of the judiciary, it is in continual jeopardy of being overpowered, awed, or influenced by its co-ordinate branches; and that as nothing can contribute so much to its firmness and independence as permanency in office, this quality may therefore be justly regarded as an indispensable ingredient in its constitution, and, in a great measure, as the citadel of the public justice and the public security.[60]

Political leaders need to be careful about fundamentally altering the US Supreme Court for purely partisan reasons, because once the pandora's box is open, every time Democrats or Republicans gain control of all three branches of government, there will be strong push to reshape the court in their image. This was one of the fears our Founders had about unbridled power being a clear threat to our constitutional republic.

Our founders also enshrined in the US Constitution the president's sole responsibility in conducting US foreign policy, but placed a check on his authority, by giving the US Congress a role in oversite, funding, and the ability to declare war. The Senate had the constitutional mandates in approving nominations to fill various executive agencies and other positions. The Seante also has constitutional responsibility in ratifying all treaties. This aspect has been relegated to mute. During the Obama presidency, agreements were signed, such as the UN Climate Change Conference (COP21) or what it's commonly known as The Paris Climate agreement and the Joint Comprehensive Plan of Action (JCPOA) or the Iran nuclear deal. Both were agreements only and never ratified by the Seante.

Since the end of the Cold War, each Republican and Democrat president has campaigned on purely a domestic agenda with virtually no national security vision on what role America plays in global affairs. Far too often, each Democrat and Republican president regularly react to events instead of shaping a coherent national security strategy.

In 2020, the late Anthony H. Cordesman of The Center for Strategic and International Studies wrote a report in which he stated:

> The US has made progress in one area: making increases in the defense budget, but far too many of these increases have gone to funding the readiness and the shopping lists of the US military services. There have been few original ideas and changes that have actually benefitted America's national security.
>
> The US still lurches from one budget year to the next budget year with no clear path for shaping its strategy, planning programing, or shift in direction that goes beyond past underfunding or near-term reactions to events. The US has failed to build effectively on its new National Security Strategy (NSS) issued in 2017. The new strategy was only the rough shell of a real strategy when it was initially issued, and it has never been turned into real plans or any consistent effort at implementation.[61]

With the Cold War a distant memory, and the US coming out of twenty years of endless wars throughout the Middle East, America needs a president to set a clear foreign policy vision upon entering the White House. Currently, the US faces a resurgent Russia trying to reclaim past glories, an aggressive China pursuing the goal of supplanting the US as the world's dominate power, Iran — whose ambition is to be the dominate power in the Middle East, and fermenting armed conflict across the Middle East in its quest to push the US out of the region. As I mentioned in the introduction, since the end of the Cold War, America hasn't had a clear direction of what role the United States plays in world affairs. With the end of America's twenty-year wars across the Middle East, what is America's global vision?

America is facing challenges unseen in its history. During the Cold War, it was threats from Russia that consumed the US. Now, the United States is facing threats from a variety of nations, and one that is more reminiscent of the great power competition of the nineteenth century.

After the end of World War II, the United States played a clear role in establishing a liberal economic system where free trade and commerce to benefit the global community. Today, the American people don't understand why the US must be involved in all international upheavals. The American people were clear in the 2024 presidential election. They want Washington to spend its efforts in improving the economic lives of Americans and not send billions to other nations around the world.

America hasn't come to grips with its role in global affairs. Explain this to the American people. Today, the US sees billions going to other countries, such as Ukraine, Israel, and Africa, while Americans are suffering at home. How do you explain to the American people the war in Ukraine, Gaza, Lebanon, and Africa are directly linked and impact the American economy? It has been decades since a president has set forth a comprehensive national security strategy which encompasses all aspects of US executive agencies into a robust strategy.

The first step in developing a strategy is to plan goals and objectives. Traditionally, most American presidents have implemented a national security strategy based upon their "political agenda and to promote their party's philosophy of governing." Because the plan is politically motivated and lacks details about how the goals will be achieved, the result is often ineffective or inconsequential. Coupled with a "geographically defined representative legislature," it is difficult to identify "what the country will not do as a nation" in maintaining national security.

The greatest challenge for the United States is that it "lacks the government structure to develop" a national security strategy. Hyper-partisan congressional committees and subcommittees, each working within their individual spheres of control, make it nearly impossible for a comprehensive national security strategy to come out of the legislative branch. The constitution places the executive branch, namely the president, in charge of foreign affairs and national security. However, the executive branch is divided into cabinet departments with different operational jurisdictions and personalities. This predicament was explained in a 2024 report by the Center for Strategic & International Studies (CSIS).

> Within the White House, the president has a National Security Council and a National Economic Council, each competing for the president's time and focus. Important elements of the US economy—such as US universities and research institutions—have only a weak channel into the most senior levels of decision making in the White House. In short, the country lacks a structural focus for creating a new national strategy.
>
> To develop a new national strategy, we return to the fundamental mission statement for the US government from the Constitution: to survive as a nation and to prosper as a people.
>
> Security is a prerequisite for prosperity, and prosperity is required to support the structures of government that guarantee security. As stated by a wise observer, "We must be safe before we can get rich, and we must get rich to remain safe."[62]

The Trump administration's new national security strategy relies on the Constitution for its mission statement: "to establish Justice, ensure domestic Tranquility, provide for the common defense, promote the general Welfare, and secure the Blessings of Liberty to ourselves and our Posterity." For the Department of Defense, its mission is clear: deter war and protect the homeland.

President Trump's administration has vowed to overhaul all aspects of US national security with a strong emphasis on placing America first. One of these areas is maintaining strong national defense. We will be discussing this in greater depth in subsequent chapters, but serious examination must address the enormous amount of money spent on the US military. Is the money allocated correctly and are we spending in the right way?

The new administration must address the mission requirements that were not around decades ago. The last major overhaul of the Defense Department was in the 1980s, some forty years ago. At the time, there was no Cyber Command, space-based resources were in its infancy. US intelligence has grown significantly, mainly because of September 11, 2001, with a lot of the growth of intelligence embedded in the Department of Defense. More detail on restoring American deterrence as it relates to the Department of Defense will be discussed in subsequent chapters.

The president needs to put forth a comprehensive national security strategy that encompasses all aspects of US of national power. It should fully integrate every executive agency into a coherent strategy and not rely solely on a military first response to events. Congress also will have a role in advising and passing many aspects of US national security legislation. Over the decades, Congress has abdicated its congressional authority over conflict intervention to the executive branch.

In our hyper-partisan world, the various House and Senate committees have diverged. Political parties attack whatever party controls the executive branch instead of working together to put forth a comprehensive national security strategy. The Armed Services and Foreign Affairs Committees in both the Senate as well as The House of Representatives have oversite over US Foreign Affairs and National Defense. They need to ask relevant questions devoid of any partisan agenda or to score cheap political points. This was never more evident than during the Iraq and Afghanistan conflicts, despite members of both Democrats and Republicans supporting these conflicts. This questioning also extends to asking substantive questions about military policy and the strategy of senior military commanders. When the Chairman of the Joint Chiefs of Staff and others come before the House and Senate Committees, questions need to be asked, and these military leaders must understand they are swearing an oath to the constitution to give their best military advice.

Congress must understand its constitutional role in oversite and advise and consent. They must not accept regurgitated talking points of the administration unless they agree with the decision the president has made. What we have been doing over the past few decades hasn't worked. Congress really needs to dial down on clear answers to some of these pressing issues and not have a bias.

Ironically, members of Congress are fond of criticizing the Administration for lacking a strategy. Congress, however, can be criticized for failing to insist on adequate reporting of wartime budgets and examining their costs in detail. Aside from independent efforts by the Congressional Research Service (CRS), neither the Executive Branch nor the Congress have ever issued an official report on the costs of American's ongoing wars, examined the trends in these costs, or insisted on meaningful reporting on their effectiveness.[63]

The US still hasn't come to grips on a true bipartisan investigation to what happened during the chaotic and disastrous withdrawal from Afghanistan. The broader question which needs to be asked is: What led up to this debacle in Afghanistan? We had twenty years of war, then as soon as we pulled out, the entire country collapsed. Over the past twenty years military and national security leaders routinely testified on Capitol Hill, stating we were making progress. How did it turn so wrong? Why was the US State Department so ill-prepared for the withdrawal? The American people, and more importantly, US service personnel who sacrificed everything, need to know what happened.

The final thing in America's dysfunctional political system is one that is often referred as the "fourth branch of government." That is the complete bias by the mainstream media. Instead of fact-based reporting, journalists have now obliterated their own journalistic ethics and are focused on advocacy journalism. Truth and fact have been shunned in favor of advocacy journalism, focusing on tipping the scale in favor of one political party; namely the Democratic Party. Just examine what is being taught throughout our college and university system, as advocacy journalism is the central focus of instruction at college and university journalistic programs.

Many will see this as political bias on my part, but objectively examine how Republicans are treated verse how Democrats are covered. George Washington University Constitutional Law Professor Law Professor Jonathan Turley discusses this in great depth in his book, *The Indispensable Right, Free Speech in an Age of Rage*.

One excellent resource for determining biased from nonbiased reporting is provided by the *Society of Professional Journalists*. Reproduced here with their permission, this invaluable resource thoroughly defines and explains ethical journalism. Their website, 'https://www.spj.org/', provides additional resources and information.

Society of Professional Journalists
C*SPJ*DE *of* ETHICS

PREAMBLE

Members of the Society of Professional Journalists believe that public enlightenment is the forerunner of justice and the foundation of democracy. Ethical journalism strives to ensure the free exchange of information that is accurate, fair and thorough. An ethical journalist acts with integrity.

The Society declares these four principles as the foundation of ethical journalism and encourages their use in its practice by all people in all media.

SEEK TRUTH AND REPORT IT

Ethical journalism should be accurate and fair. Journalists should be honest and courageous in gathering, reporting and interpreting information.

Journalists should:

- Take responsibility for the accuracy of their work. Verify information before releasing it. Use original sources whenever possible.
- Remember that neither speed nor format excuses inaccuracy.
- Provide context. Take special care not to misrepresent or oversimplify in promoting, previewing or summarizing a story.
- Gather, update and correct information throughout the life of a news story.
- Be cautious when making promises, but keep the promises they make.
- Identify sources clearly. The public is entitled to as much information as possible to judge the reliability and motivations of sources.
- Consider sources' motives before promising anonymity. Reserve anonymity for sources who may face danger, retribution or other harm, and have information that cannot be obtained elsewhere. Explain why anonymity was granted.
- Diligently seek subjects of news coverage to allow them to respond to criticism or allegations of wrongdoing.
- Avoid undercover or other surreptitious methods of gathering information unless traditional, open methods will not yield information vital to the public.
- Be vigilant and courageous about holding those with power accountable. Give voice to the voiceless.
- Support the open and civil exchange of views, even views they find repugnant.
- Recognize a special obligation to serve as watchdogs over public affairs and government. Seek to ensure that the public's business is conducted in the open, and that public records are open to all.
- Provide access to source material when it is relevant and appropriate.
- Boldly tell the story of the diversity and magnitude of the human experience. Seek sources whose voices we seldom hear.
- Avoid stereotyping. Journalists should examine the ways their values and experiences may shape their reporting.
- Label advocacy and commentary.
- Never deliberately distort facts or context, including visual information. Clearly label illustrations and re-enactments.
- Never plagiarize. Always attribute.

MINIMIZE HARM

Ethical journalism treats sources, subjects, colleagues and members of the public as human beings deserving of respect.

Journalists should:

- Balance the public's need for information against potential harm or discomfort. Pursuit of the news is not a license for arrogance or undue intrusiveness.
- Show compassion for those who may be affected by news coverage. Use heightened sensitivity when dealing with juveniles, victims of sex crimes, and sources or subjects who are inexperienced or unable to give consent. Consider cultural differences in approach and treatment.
- Recognize that legal access to information differs from an ethical justification to publish or broadcast.
- Realize that private people have a greater right to control information about themselves than public figures and others who seek power, influence or attention. Weigh the consequences of publishing or broadcasting personal information.
- Avoid pandering to lurid curiosity, even if others do.
- Balance a suspect's right to a fair trial with the public's right to know. Consider the implications of identifying criminal suspects before they face legal charges.
- Consider the long-term implications of the extended reach and permanence of publication. Provide updated and more complete information as appropriate.

ACT INDEPENDENTLY

The highest and primary obligation of ethical journalism is to serve the public.

Journalists should:

- Avoid conflicts of interest, real or perceived. Disclose unavoidable conflicts.
- Refuse gifts, favors, fees, free travel and special treatment, and avoid political and other outside activities that may compromise integrity or impartiality, or may damage credibility.
- Be wary of sources offering information for favors or money; do not pay for access to news. Identify content provided by outside sources, whether paid or not.
- Deny favored treatment to advertisers, donors or any other special interests, and resist internal and external pressure to influence coverage.
- Distinguish news from advertising and shun hybrids that blur the lines between the two. Prominently label sponsored content.

BE ACCOUNTABLE AND TRANSPARENT

Ethical journalism means taking responsibility for one's work and explaining one's decisions to the public.

Journalists should:

- Explain ethical choices and processes to audiences. Encourage a civil dialogue with the public about journalistic practices, coverage and news content.
- Respond quickly to questions about accuracy, clarity and fairness.
- Acknowledge mistakes and correct them promptly and prominently. Explain corrections and clarifications carefully and clearly.
- Expose unethical conduct in journalism, including within their organizations.
- Abide by the same high standards they expect of others.

The SPJ Code of Ethics is a statement of abiding principles supported by additional explanations and position papers (at spj.org) that address changing journalistic practices. It is not a set of rules, rather a guide that encourages all who engage in journalism to take responsibility for the information they provide, regardless of medium. The code should be read as a whole; individual principles should not be taken out of context. It is not, nor can it be under the First Amendment, legally enforceable.

https://www.spj.org/spj-code-of-ethics/ [64]

Just examine the Harvard commencement address in June of 1978, by Russian dissident Aleksandr Solzhenitsyn.

> Here again, the main concern is not to infringe the letter of the law. There is no true moral responsibility for deformation or disproportion. What sort of responsibility does a journalist, or a newspaper have to his readers, or to his history—or to history? If they have misled public opinion or the government by inaccurate information or wrong conclusions, do we know of any cases of public recognition and rectification of such mistakes by the same journalist

or the same newspaper? It hardly ever happens because it would damage sales. A nation may be the victim of such a mistake, but the journalist usually always gets away with it. One may—One may safely assume that he will start writing the opposite with renewed self-assurance.

Because instant and credible information has to be given, it becomes necessary to resort to guesswork, rumors, and suppositions to fill in the voids, and none of them will ever be rectified; they will stay on in the readers' memories. How many hasty, immature, superficial, and misleading judgments are expressed every day, confusing readers, without any verification? The press—The press can both simulate public opinion and mis-educate it. Thus, we may see terrorists described as heroes, or secret matters pertaining to one's nation's defense publicly revealed, or we may witness shameless intrusion on the privacy of well-known people under the slogan: "Everyone is entitled to know everything." But this is a false slogan, characteristic of a false era. People also have the right not to know and it's a much more valuable one. The right not to have their divine souls [stuffed with gossip, nonsense, vain talk.] A person who works and leads a meaningful life does not need this excessive burdening flow of information.[65]

Just examine the abuses by the media over the past few years, openly colluding with then-President Joe Biden, in censoring what the American people viewed, heard and read. Just examine some of the major news stories the mainstream media got wrong or badly misrepresented as fact.

Start with the Russian collusion narrative, where the mainstream media accused and actively reported that then-Republican presidential candidate, Donald Trump, in 2016, colluded with Russia to win the presidency. When in fact, Democratic presidential Candidate Hillary Clinton, in her paranoid manner, was attempting to take the heat off her email scandal where she had all classified materials sent to her private email account. Clinton used the law firm, Perkins Coi, which used the intelligence firm, Fusion GPS, for opposition research that hired a foreign intelligence operative, Christopher Steele, who also happened to be a paid informant of the FBI, under then Director James Comey. This unique collaboration fabricated the "Steele Dossier" which was the foundation of instigating the Russian collusion investigation of then-candidate, Donald Trump.

This was peddled around throughout the government, working with the mainstream media and social media companies, pushed illegal information to the FISA courts to get a surveillance warrant, had a forged FBI document submitted as factual evidence.

> Two years later, the self-congratulatory Robert Mueller's "dream team" and "all-stars" of liberal beltway lawyers evaporated after finding no such Trump-Russian collusion—after a wasted nearly two years and $40 million. Meanwhile, revelations emerged of all sorts of covert FBI skullduggery— from erasing incriminating cell phone records, the revelations of the Strzok-Page text exchanges indicating an apparent FBI "insurance policy" effort to preclude a winning Trump candidacy, to the meltdown of Director Comey himself, who lied to the president that he was not a target of an investigation and then leaked confidential records of a private one-on-one presidential conversation to the media.[66]

Over the next two years, this narrative fell apart even after then Special Counsel Robert Mueller and his many constitutional judicial legal teams found no evidence of any Russian collusion by the Donald Trump or anyone on his presidential campaign. What we did learn during the Russian collusion investigation is all manner of unethical if not illegal practices by the FBI such as erasing incriminating cell phone records, the revelations of the Strzok-Page text exchanges indicating an apparent FBI "insurance policy" effort to preclude a winning Trump candidacy, to the meltdown of Director Comey himself, who lied to the president that he was not a target of an investigation and then leaked confidential records of a private one-on-one presidential conversation to the media. The media relentlessly pushed this false narrative and two major news organizations, the New York Times and The Washington Post, received the coveted journalistic award: The Pulitzer Prize, for their Russian Collusion narrative. This was all based on a lie!

The second major story was at the final stages of the 2020 presidential election, where every news organization suppressed a New York Post story regarding then former Vice President Joe Biden's son Hunter's laptop which contained massive amounts of documents show vast array of foreign business dealings which resulted in payments to the Biden family.

A later 2020 campaign effort jumpstarted by the current Biden Secretary of State Antony Blinken and the former interim CIA Director Mike Morrell, with help from former CIA Directors John Brennan and Leon Panetta, along with former Director of National Intelligence James Clapper, to round up 51 "former" (but actually many enjoying then-current CIA contractor status) "intelligence authorities" to publicly mislead the public by signing a letter that the incriminating Hunter Biden laptop (then in the hands of and authenticated as genuine by the FBI) was once again a Russian effort to throw the election to Trump. It was an obvious scripted lie, but timely scheduled before the last debate to arm Biden with plausible denials and thus to help swing the election to him. And it likely did.[67]

Since this eventually proved true, the media had no interest in investigating, despite the many lies by Joe Biden on his having no knowledge of his son's business dealings. In December 2024, the National Archives produced a photo of Joe Biden, Hunter Biden, and his Chinese business associates. Remember, Biden stated he never met with his son's business associates. The media just let this pass.

How about an effort by the heads of the NIH, Francis Collins, and NIAID, Anthony Fauci, deliberately to obfuscate, and allegedly in the case of Fauci, to lie under oath, about the efforts of American health authorities?

. . . to evade US prohibitions on gain-in-function viral research, by funding the third-party EcoHealth Alliance to facilitate the transference of American money, instrumentation, and consulting to partner with the Chinese communist Wuhan virology lab; 2) to obfuscate the truth that the lab had somehow leaked the lethal, manmade virus—birthed with the help of US expertise—that was killing millions worldwide; 3) to promulgate a false scenario of a bat/pangolin origin; 4) to deny under oath the American government's role in the birth of the virus; 5) to suppress dissident scientific voices; and 6) to advise radical quarantine policies that would virtually destroy the US economy along with the Trump 2020 reelection effort, and then shift blame from their own culpability to a false narrative that Trump was the chief driver of a disastrous national shutdown that had ruined the economy and yet was supposedly nearly criminally lax in controlling the outbreak.[68]

The media has also failed to investigate the massive censorship operation, where the Biden administration perpetrated the largest censorship operation in US history. The administration worked, and in some cases, forced the social media companies to censor opposing viewpoints. US District Judge Terry Doughty of Louisiana remarked that this court case had "Orwellian" aspect as it relates to the Biden censorship operation by forcing social media censor contents they disagreed with.

What about President Biden's obvious cognitive decline, which was visible to all? The mainstream media initially failed to report on, and only began to cover it when Biden had the disastrous debate with Donald Trump — it became too incredulous to cover up. In December of 2024, the Wall Street Journal wrote a piece about how the White House staff and close advisor hid the fact of his cognitive decline. The White House staff controlled his every move, including who he met with, and controlled his access to the media and the American people, beginning just a few months into his administration.

In 2021, Democratic Representative Adam Smith was the Chairman of the House Armed Services Committee and spent months trying to get in touch with Biden, to no avail. This was at a time the US was preparing to pull out of Afghanistan. Even Democratic Rep. Jim Himes, Ranking Member on the House Permanent Select Committee on Intelligence, had difficulty meeting with the president. This at the time of the Russian-Ukraine conflict and the wars in the Middle East. President Biden was absent and in obvious cognitive decline. No one asked if the president was up to the job. Nor did they care to ask the most important question: Who was making key policies if the president was not up to the job?

This is only a small sampling of the bias of the media. Does anyone wonder why trust in the media is at an all-time low?

Four

American Diplomacy Resurrected

If America is going to have a strong foreign policy, then it needs a proper US Department of State to lead such efforts. Since the terror attacks on September 11, 2001, the United States has engaged in twenty years of perpetual armed conflict throughout the Middle East, and during this time, other areas of the globe received less attention. With America entering a "great power competition," it will now require a different approach than solely a military solution.

The US now faces a different kind of international arena, one more reminiscent of the great power competition of the 19th century.

The United States enjoyed unrivaled supremacy in the two decades after the end of the Cold War, with relative and absolute military and economic capabilities that far outstripped those of any other world power. This position of extraordinary privilege allowed it to pursue policies without worrying too much about how they were viewed by or affected other world powers. Primacy was a strategic luxury that permitted the United States to adopt a transformative foreign policy agenda aimed at building a liberal world order with itself at the center. This approach initially had a strategic logic behind it and achieved a great deal of good. The United States helped to stabilize the war-torn Balkans in the 1990s and increased the chances that democracy would take root in Central and Eastern Europe. Hundreds of millions of people around the world were lifted out of poverty in this period.

> Yet the same strategic luxury also permitted Washington to pursue a far-ranging global campaign in the wake of the September 11, 2001, terrorist attacks that led it to commit the strategic blunder of invading Iraq and turned a targeted anti–al Qaeda campaign in Afghanistan into a nation-building operation that ultimately failed. It also led to overreach in Europe and set the stage for overreach in Asia.[69]

Far too often, the US looks at foreign policy issues through the guise of only utilizing a military approach first, and less at utilizing all elements of national power. The famed Prussian military theorist Carl von Clausewitz wrote in his famous book, *On War*, that war is the continuation of politics by other means. In essence, when all other options fail then the military solution is the method used to achieve the desired political outcome.

If the US is to function effectively in the multi-complex international environment, it will need a robust and effective Department of State, one that is not encumbered by a complex bureaucracy and political divisions within its ranks. Before any reform can take place, questions must be asked. The US must articulate "a coherent vision of the State Department's proper role in the US national security apparatus. Should the Department of State assume the role of lead designer of US foreign policy? Or should it defer strategic thinking to the National Security Council and others, and focus more on the execution of US foreign policy?"

Is the state department's job to direct policy or to carry it out? While attempting to do both, they are ineffective at either. This dichotomy is one of the main problems facing the State Department today. For too long, efforts have been placed on the academic side, without truly examining how those academic strategies actually fit into what is truly happening on the ground in the real world. One major problem is that the staff of the State Department are recruited mainly from the academic world and the field is devoid of individuals who are not raised and born into the culture of a given area. The State Department would be more effective if they would recruit outside of Washington and traditional academic colleges and universities. An academic education should not be the sole litmus test of who is employed at the State Department. Far too often, they overlook those who do not have a traditional academic degree but have worldwide experience. Worldwide life experience is just as valuable as academic credentials.[70]

The State Department has another key problem. In 2010, then-Sen. Kent Conrad, D-ND, proposed a $4 billion reduction in its budget. He received pushback from two key allies who surprisingly came from an unlikely source: the Department of Defense. Then Chairman of The Joint Chiefs of Staff Admiral Michael Mullen wrote, "We are living in times that require an integrated national security program with budgets that fund the full spectrum of national security efforts, including vitally important pre-conflict and post-conflict civilian stabilization programs. Diplomatic programs are critical to our long-term security."[71]

At the same time, Secretary of Defense Robert Gates penned a letter to Democratic US Senator Ken Conrad of North Dakota who was a ranking member of the Seante Budget committee and was in favor of reducing the State Department's budget.

> I understand this year presents a challenging budget environment, with competing domestic and international pressures. However, I strongly believe a robust civilian foreign affairs capability, coupled with a strong defense capability, is essential to preserving US national security interests around the world.
>
> State and USAID partners are critical to success in Afghanistan, Pakistan, and Iraq. Our military and civilian missions are integrated, and we depend upon our civilian counterparts to help stabilize and rebuild after the fight. As US forces transition out of war zones, the US government needs our civilian agencies to be able to assume critical functions. This allows us, for example, to draw down US forces in Iraq responsibly while ensuring hard-fought gains are secured. Cuts will almost certainly impact our efforts in these critical frontline states.[72]

Gates even mentioned that American foreign policy has become to military centric and forced to conduct missions that it never was intended to perform, such as nation-building in Iraq and Afghanistan. The US Defense Department receives massive amounts of revenue, but unfortunately The Department of State receives crumbs, and is still expected to carry out US foreign policy.

It has become an article of faith among policymakers that principled American leadership has waned but remains in demand around the world. Moreover, America's network of international relationships is its foremost strategic asset, even as the agency charged with advancing US interests through diplomacy—the Department of State (DOS)— has fallen into a deep and sustained period of crisis. However, there is a third framing assumption: that the current crisis offers an opportunity to address this predicament and revitalize American diplomacy. "Despite the decades-long failure to implement essential reforms—and even in the face of sustained hostility from the current administration—diplomacy remains the best tool the United States has to advance its foreign policy interests."[73]

In the age of great power conflict, the United States will need diplomacy to be at the forefront of American foreign policy, and this means a robust Department of State that is well suited and prepared for the challenges in the twenty-first century. Since September 11, 2001, The United States has relied more and more on its military to fight the wars in Iraq and Afghanistan and leveraged the Department of Defense to be the lead element in its fight against international terrorism. Now that the wars in Iraq and Afghanistan have ended, the US faces the ascension of China trying to supplant America as the world's dominant power. Russia has renewed aggression in its attempt to recapture its former glory. Iran is fermenting aggression throughout the Middle East, and more and more countries are joining the original BRIC nations of Brazil, Russia, India, and China.

> To some in the West, the emergence of BRICS+ suggests something even more ominous—a world that is fragmenting into competing blocs, thanks to intensifying geopolitical rivalry between East and West and growing mutual alienation between North and South. According to this reading, Beijing and Moscow are intent on exploiting some countries' resentment of the United States and its wealthy world allies to consolidate an anti-Western counterweight to the venerable Group of 7 (G7), a process that is likely to paralyze global cooperation within other multilateral venues. Of particular concern is the future of the Group of 20 (G20). Even before BRICS expansion, it had become a microcosm of growing global rifts. A further hardening of these divisions would undercut the G20's fundamental raison d'être: namely,

to help bridge gulfs between—and leverage the capabilities of—important countries that are not inherently or necessarily like-minded.[74]

President Trump has vowed to do everything in his power to put United States citizens first by ensuring their protection and opportunity to prosper. Globally, America's priority should be to promote the common good. "This will require a United States that acts in solidarity with others, considers the effects of American foreign policy on people around the world, and seeks to promote US security and prosperity while not exporting insecurity and economic precarity onto them."[75]

For the United States to be effective in the new global arena and in the new great power competition, it will need to take a different approach to foreign policy. Far too often, the foreign policy establishment from both Republican and Democrats have relied on utilizing the military option as the only solution and lead with a military-centric approach. The US needs a different approach.

Unlike in the past, America's power is not unlimited and has been diminishing over the decades. With the largest economy and the most advanced military in the world, the US has the ability to assert power anywhere in the world. The US needs to be judicious about how that power is utilized, as its power can shape the global agenda for all to benefit, and be the bullwork against the various authoritative countries who are trying to upend that world order, most notably China. "Addressing urgent common challenges requires a nuanced approach to recognizing that global engagement is vital not only to defending liberal values and human security but also to assuring each country's prosperity."[76]

The United States fails to utilize all elements of its national power. This is one of the weaknesses of United States foreign policy since the end of the Cold War that has changed since the terror attack on September 11. The US needs to use its immense economic and political power in dealing with international challenges. As military theorist Carl Von Clausewitz summarizes his treatise on the beginning of conflict, "No one starts a war — or rather, no one in his senses ought to do so — without first being clear in his mind what he intends to achieve by that war and how he intends to conduct it." American national security professionals need to remember this military axiom.

This statement by Clausewitz, encapsulates what is wrong with US foreign policy. Far too often, presidents of both political parties have utilized the military first option and sent America into conflicts without fully articulating a coherent strategy on what they were trying to accomplish.[77]

The famous British leader, Winston Churchill, remarked on the beginning of a conflict, "Never, never, never believe any war will be smooth and easy, or that anyone who embarks on that strange voyage can measure the tides and hurricanes he will encounter. The Statesman who yields to war fever must realize that once the signal is given, he is no longer the Master of Policy but the slave of unforeseeable and uncontrollable events...."[78] President Trump's administration came into office facing a far different world than the one he bequeathed to his successor President Joe Biden. America's humiliating withdrawal and the chaos it created had global implications that many may not want to admit. Russia's President Vladimir Putin used American weakness to invade Ukraine and remain committed to continuing the onslaught of destruction in that country without fear of the United States. The Middle East is in a blaze of destruction with wars breaking out across the region, with Iran fermenting most of this destruction. China, Russia, and Iran have formed the new *Tripartite Pact*, which was a defensive alliance signed by Germany, Japan, and Italy.

Many traditional United States allies are worried about our staying power. China's aggression in the Indo-Pacific region was met with an unimpressive response from America. Beijing is making major inroads into Latin America. Even the Monroe Doctrine is facing major encroachment by China's Belt and Road Initiative. US foreign policy needs a major change that utilizes all of America's national power.

As of this writing, national security experts have argued that the United States needs a strategic recalibration of its entire foreign policy apparatus. Unlike in the past, the US needs to be more "selective in its commitments and engagements if it is to remain secure and prosperous in the decades to come." The Trump administration received a tectonic push back from the national security community on how he is dealing with our adversaries and his often-tense relationships with our long-time allies. President Trump believes that the past twenty years has stretched America and tangled the US in endless wars with little to show for our efforts in blood and treasure. The US must understand we are still the dominant power, but America now faces a multipolar world and the nation cannot afford a policy of largesse everywhere at all times. The US cannot withdraw from the world, as the US has many global commitments. An isolationist America will only leave authoritative nations such as China to fill the vacuum.

> This legacy leaves the United States with an approach to the world that is poorly adapted to the challenges of today and tomorrow. US officials have long been concerned about the rise of China and a revanchist Russia, but they focused on other issues until recently. Avoiding the realities of America's relative decline in power and legitimacy has come back to bite the United States since the mid-2010s, when Russian President Vladimir Putin launched the war on Ukraine and Chinese President Xi Jinping put the country on a more nationalist and assertive course. The United States now faces a more multipolar world than ever in its history as the world's leading power. In the coming decades, great-power dynamics will decide fundamental matters of war and peace, prosperity, and security, and cooperation and competition. This emerging new international reality, coupled with the dismaying outcomes of US wars in Iraq and Afghanistan, suggests that the country would benefit if it could reform and update its approach to the world. Doing so, however, will be exceedingly difficult.[79]

If the US State Department is to lead US foreign policy, pursuant to the direction put forth by the President of the United States, it needs major reform to effect this change in a challenging new international environment.

In 2020, The Council on Foreign Relations put forth a report on the deficiency encapsulated in the US State Department.

> The most pressing challenges facing the State Department include a twenty-first century policy environment that has, in some priority evolved beyond the core competencies of most Foreign and Civil Service officers and an institution hollowed out by three years of talent flight, mired in excessively layered structure, and resistant to reform. Perhaps most important, they

include the multigenerational challenge of a diplomatic workforce that falls woefully short of reflecting the diverse country it serves, particularly at the senior-most ranks, compromising its effectiveness and fostering a homogeneous and risk-averse culture that drives out rather than cultivates fresh perspectives. The State Department today risks losing the "war for talent," not only to the private sector but increasingly to other government agencies, due to inflexible career tracks, self-defeating hiring constraints, and a lack of commitment to training and professional development. Finally, DOS is hampered by Congress's failure over many years to pass authorizing legislation, leading to budgetary pressures and diminishing DOS's status in the hierarchy of national security agencies rather than reinforcing the nation's paramount foreign policy institution.

The State Department needs to hire talented workers with skills in a variety of areas. Top-tier talent must be recruited from outside the agency. Academic degrees are not the only metric for education. Just because someone doesn't have a formal degree does not mean they cannot offer expertise and knowledge. "This will include both returning to the essentials of diplomatic tradecraft — grounded in doctrine, case studies, and professional education — and extending them to the areas that will define the State Department's work in the decades ahead."[80]

For reform to be initiated, the State Department will have to examine and recalibrate how it brings on talent into the foreign service and civil service system. An excellent place to begin this reform is to examine history, starting with William J. Donovan, who established the Office of Strategic Services (OSS) during World War II. Donovan created America's true intelligence agency and later become the father of the Central Intelligence Agency (CIA). This is all laid out in his biography, *America's Master Spy*, written by Richard Dunlop in 2014.

One of Donovan's key tenants was to hire anyone with the resident talent useful in intelligence gathering. Strange as it may be, this approach can also work for the State Department. Donovan would hire not only someone coming from elite colleges and universities, but would utilize individuals in businesses and various legal firms. Ironically, Donovon hired numerous women into the OSS, which was unheard of at the time. The State Department needs to look at diversity in its hiring practices, but not in the vein of Diversity, Equity, and Inclusion (DEI). Eliminate DEI and hire the best candidate for the position, regardless of demographic. This means looking at a candidate who has expertise in a region. Perhaps they were not born in the US or they graduated from a lesser-known college or university. The ideal candidate brings a wealth of experience into the State Department. Have an independent mechanism set up if this is not happening.

Many of the vast numbers of individuals hired by Donovon were not prominent nor held any high social standing. The State Department also needs to look at bringing on foreign émigrés who not only have language expertise but understand the culture nuances. This skill is often missing from those who study language at college or university. These foreign émigrés can bring greater clarity of the region and truly understand the culture dynamics because they were born into culture. This was one of America's greatest flaws as we became involved in armed conflict in Iraq and Afghanistan, but especially Afghanistan. We had virtually no one who spoke the language or the various dialects, or understood the vast tribal dynamics.

Donovan had obtained the support of the Librarian of Congress, poet Archibald MacLeish, to allow the prospective organization to use the library's extensive materials in analyzing the Axis' strengths and weaknesses. In July, Donovan hired the President of Williams College, James Phinney Baxter III, an historian, to head the COI's Research and Analysis (R&A) Branch. Baxter and Donovan quickly recruited noted scholars in various disciplines from prestigious colleges and universities and put them to work in the Library of Congress. Among the early recruits were Harvard historian William L. Langer; Edward Meade Earle from the Institute for Advanced Study in Princeton; economist Edward S. Mason from Harvard; Joseph Hayden, a University of Michigan political scientist and former vice governor of the Philippines; historian Sherman Kent of Yale; Wilmarth S. Lewis, millionaire Yale biographer of Horace Walpole; and James L. McConaughy, President of Wesleyan University, and many others. Within a few months, Donovan began sending to Roosevelt summaries of detailed R&A reports on strategic economic, political, social, and military information about conditions and strategic prospects in Europe, North Africa, and the Middle East. Robert E. Sherwood, noted playwright, pacifist turned interventionist and a speech writer for the President, enthusiastically endorsed the idea of undermining enemy morale and bolstering resistance via short-wave radio broadcasts and other media aimed at Nazi Germany and German-occupied countries, and Donovan quickly chose him to head COI's Foreign Information Service. Within a few months, Donovan added a Visual Presentation Branch, which would include Hollywood directors John Ford, famous for his westerns and other epics, and Merian C. Cooper, adventurer/filmmaker and creator of King Kong.[81]

One of the strategic failures of the United States, one which Donovan would have rejected, was the elimination of the United States Information Agency (USIA) in the name of budgetary cuts as outdated as a Cold War relic. The USIA was established during the presidency of Dwight Eisenhower with the mission: "to understand, inform and influence foreign publics in promotion of the national interest, and to broaden the dialogue between Americans and US institutions, and their counterparts abroad."[82]

A perfect example of a missed opportunity was in 2002, when the United States sent relief aid to Iran after a devastating earthquake. President George W. Bush stated, "Human suffering knows no political boundaries." This would have been a perfect opportunity for USIA, if it was still in existence, to provide relief to the suffering people of Iran during this horrific earthquake. Instead, the Iranian people formed a one-sided demonic view of the United States.

This agency also could have been used during the COVID-19 pandemic by relaying to the Iranian people that the virus, which was unleashed by China, which killed close to 150,000 people in Iran. USIA could have targeted Iran with information that the Iranian government is selling energy to China, a country responsible for the deaths of upward of 150,00 Iranians.[83]

As America begins to come to grips with a multipolar world, it is inevitable that China will continue to be a driving force in foreign policy decisions. Other "areas of focus will include India, the world's largest democracy; Southeast Asia, a bastion of global economic growth; the Western Hemisphere, home to America's primary trading partners and the source of a migration and humanitarian crisis and a policy crisis at the US-Mexico border; and Nigeria, Africa's most populous country and largest economy."

Africa is now playing out as the recreation of the great game of the nineteenth century, as both Russia and China are now vying for the continent's valuable rare earth minerals. In the coming decades, the continent will have a young and growing population. The US State Department will need to recalibrate in order to "manage these strategic relationships and advise policymakers."[84]

With China at the forefront of US foreign policy, no matter who is president, the State Department will have to do a better job of coordinating with other agencies across the broad spectrum of national security. This also means working closely with the Department of Defense and avoiding the adversarial relationship that existed in the past. The State Department will be the lead entity in conducting US foreign policy with the hammer confined to the Department of Defense. The following quotes from *Mandate for Leadership: The Conservative Promise 2025* explain the significance of President Trump's foreign policy.

> Interagency engagement in this new environment must be similarly adjusted to mirror presidential direction. Indeed, coordination among federal agencies is challenging even in the most well-oiled Administrations. Although such coordination is inescapable and sometimes productive, agencies tend to leverage each other's resources in ways that occasionally have off-mission consequences for the agency or agencies with the resources. Ideally, the Secretary of State should work as part of an agile foreign policy team along with the National Security Advisor, the Secretary of Defense, and other agency heads to flesh out and advance the President's foreign policy. Bureaucratic stovepipes of the past should be less important than commitment to, and achievement of, the President's foreign policy agenda. The State Department's role in these interagency discussions must reflect the President's clear direction and disallow resources and tools to be used in any way that detracts from the presidentially directed mission.

Simultaneously, The State Department must coordinate with Congress.

> Congress has both the statutory and appropriations authority to impact the State Department's operations and has a strong interest in key aspects of American foreign policy. The department must therefore take particular care in its interaction with Congress, since poor interactions with Congress,

regardless of intentions, could trigger congressional pushbacks or have other negative impacts on the President's agenda. This will require particularly strong leadership of the Department of State's Bureau of Legislative Affairs. The Secretary of State and political leadership should ensure full coordination with the White House regarding congressional engagement on any State Department responsibility. This may lead to, for example, the President authorizing the State Department to engage with Members of Congress and relevant committees on certain issues (including statutorily designated congressional consultations), but to remain "radio silent" on volatile or designated issues on which the White House wants to be the primary or only voice. All such authorized department engagements with Congress must be driven and handled by political appointees in conjunction with career officials who have the relevant expertise and are willing to work in concert with the President's political appointees on particularly sensitive matters.[85]

With President Trump in the White House once again, and the many international challenges confronting the United States, the time is now for the US to put forth a new national security strategy that encompasses all aspects of America's national power. This will require the president, in conjunction with Congress, to forge a new direction in how it deals with China! Is China an adversary? Or are they, as President Biden once labeled them, a strategic competitor?

The State Department will need to increase the recruitment of native Chinese speakers and students enrolled in top East Asian studies, as well as individuals who know of the strategic economic, political, social, cultural, regional ethnic complexities, and military information to be infused in policy initiatives. All this needs to be infused into integrating them into briefing ambassadors and diplomats serving abroad.

The State Department needs to properly staff key positions with individuals who have expertise in their assigned country. Its ability to fill positions must not be rooted in careerism or expedience, nor should they give out preferential assignments. State Department officials assigned to the Iraq and Afghanistan conflicts were never the best or the ones with the experience to deal with the complex challenges need to further US strategies. This lack of depth of experience resulted in animosity from the Department of Defense, further eroding trust which was most needed at this critical juncture.

One of the key challenges America faces is erasing the searing images of the United States during the humiliating withdrawal from Afghanistan. This withdrawal shocked our allies around the globe. It made them wonder if America is a declining power and if China is replacing America as the dominate power. This debacle led the Russian president to believe he could invade Ukraine, and America would give a rhetorical response, as was the case during the Obama administration about the Crimea crisis in 2014. This was also amply displayed by the Obama administration in Syria when he issued his famed "redline" over Syria using chemical weapons on its own people. President Obama failed to enforce his own "redline" and thus accepted Russia's entry back into the Middle East for the first time in forty years. Many of the key national security officials were placed into key positions in the Biden administration, including Secretary of State Antony Blinken, and National Security Advisor Jake Sullivan.

One of key challenges the State Department needs to focus on is Latin America! In his December 2024 essay, *America must put the "Americas First"*, Joseph Ledford explained the importance of "America's backyard."

> Former Secretary of State George Shultz often advised, "Foreign policy starts in your own neighborhood." The United States must prioritize diplomatic relations, economic engagement, and security cooperation in the Western Hemisphere—indeed, it is foundational to the implementation of any American grand strategy designed to achieve aims of a global nature. The United States cannot successfully confront its enemies, support its allies and partners, and maintain its leading role in the world if its geopolitical neighborhood is insecure and unstable. The pursuit of regional stability, an aim enshrined in the Monroe Doctrine, has occurred in various incarnations, and the underlying strategic principle remains vital for policy makers today.
>
> Whatever threatens Latin America and the Caribbean (LAC) has an impact on American national security. "If your neighborhood is unhealthy," Shultz warned, "you're going to have all sorts of problems. "This dilemma of hemispheric security has vexed decision makers throughout the nation's

history. Even now, the formidable power of the United States does not confer complete protection within its own hemisphere. Such a paramount concern for security in the Western Hemisphere has underpinned an enduring bipartisan consensus on preserving regional stability. As a priority for policy makers, however, its significance rises and falls with each administration. For Shultz, and for President Ronald Reagan, effecting a neighborhood policy was the first order of business in foreign affairs.[86]

At the beginning of the Biden administration, President Biden pledge to do more to confront the problem dealing with illegal immigration by focusing on the countries of origin of millions of illegal migrants who try to enter the United States. Unfortunately, rhetoric never materialized into a thorough public policy in dealing with the complex challenges in Latin America and Caribbean basin. As America dithered in Latin America, China jumped into the fill the void left by the United States. Since 2000, "trade between Latin America and the Caribbean (LAC) has increased from $12 billion to $315 billion and may double in the next decade." China has also increased economic, diplomatic, and military ties with Latin America and the Caribbean, all at the expense of America.

> Inaction carries a steep price in a world of strategic competition. "The United States is present almost everywhere in the world with a lot of initiatives, but not so much in Latin America," Peruvian foreign minister Javier González-Olaechea explained to *Wall Street Journal* reporters. "It's like a very important friend who spends little time with us." Washington should take note.[87]

Joe Bruhl, a colonel in the US Army, recognized the dangers of ignoring Africa as early as 2022. His comments recommended an alternative approach toward the continent.

> America's ambivalence toward Africa puts it at a dangerous disadvantage there — and impacts US leadership around the globe. While Washington focuses on the Russian military threat in Eastern Europe and Chinese expansionism in the Pacific, Russia, and China are out-competing the United States in Africa in ways that could fundamentally alter the global balance of power.
>
> To restore momentum to its work in Africa, Washington should develop an integrated strategy that does three things: establishes continent-wide

objectives with tailored regional strategies, dramatically expands mutually beneficial economic investment, and leverages areas in which the United States holds comparative advantage over its competitors.[88]

Africa is a pivotal region for the United States. Most of the world's precious minerals used in battery production are located on the African continent. China is fully aware of this and is doing everything they can to acquire these precious minerals. Far too long. US policy has been problematic and lacked any strategic depth. The United States consistently views the African continent as a problem to be managed when situations arise, instead of seeing it as a strategic partnership.

America was forced out of Niger by the military government, which seized power in 2023—this ended the arrangement which had the military personnel and civilian staff from the US Department of Defense allowed to operate inside the country. China and Russia will fill the vacuum of US military withdrawal from Niger.

In a savvy soft-power move, China launched a 2015 initiative to put satellite televisions in 10,000 African villages. No surprise — the television sets come with free, pre-loaded access to Chinese stations, pumping state-sponsored content into homes across the continent. Today, Russia embeds a former intelligence agent as a senior defense advisor in the Central African Republic, employs the Wagner Group in Libya and elsewhere, and has deals with seven Sub-Saharan countries to build their nuclear energy infrastructure.[89]

US involvement in Africa is more than just about competing with Russia and China. It is understanding the potential of opportunity for the continent in the decades ahead. In the next thirty-five years, the African population is expected to grow. It will comprise around 30 percent of the world's population by 2055 and reach $660 by the end of this decade. In 2021, African nations initiated the African Continental Free Trade Area — essentially a free trade agreement that eliminates tariffs on 90 percent of goods, enabling raw materials to move freely, which is needed for manufacturing growth.

The last major United States initiative toward the African continent was over twenty years ago, by President George W. Bush.

At more than $5 billion a year in humanitarian aid to Africa, President Bush has given more assistance to the continent than any other president. His administration's aid was largely targeted to fight the major global health issues facing the continent: HIV/AIDS and malaria. In 2005, Bush started a $1.2 billion initiative to fight malaria. He defended the request for funding in 2007, saying, "There's no reason for little babies to be dying of mosquito bites around the world."[90]

Many Africans were excited that President Barack Obama had been elected President of the United States and were expecting great things from him, considering his ancestral home was Kenya. Unfortunately, Obama never seized on the opportunity afforded him. President Biden followed in the footsteps of his mentor, having served as his vice president. He never visited Africa during his presidency, and only set foot once on the African continent — after his Vice President Kamala Harris lost the 2024 presidential election.

Now the one region of the world that has perplexed every American president since Franklin Roosevelt is the Middle East. The problem is that each American president comes into office with the grandiose vision that they are somehow the golden child that will transform the Middle East, or are in some sort of delusional notion they will be the one to have the Israelis and Palestinians sign a Camp David type peace accord. The US needs to look at the region and its multi-complex problems, as it is and not what we hope it to be.

The United States needs to examine the leadership of the various Middle Eastern countries and examine the region from their perspectives. The leaders examine security differently than we view security. To these leaders, security is all about internal and external threats. Many of these countries were formed out of the caldron of World War I. The British and French divided up the region into their own sphere of influence, which lasted until the end of World War II, when both countries were exhausted politically, economically, and militarily, and could no longer maintain much of their empire.

The incoming Trump administration will face challenges in the Middle East unlike anything seen since 1945. The region is embroiled in a slow-motion, high-intensity war that blazes across vast geographies and involves multiple traditional partners and non-state actors. During the past year,

American military personnel have often found themselves in combat with Iranian proxies who launched a stream of missiles and drones against US and partner civilian and military shipping. ISIS is a shadow of its former self, but shows troubling signs of expansion. However, Trump strategists, our regional partners, and adversaries also operate in a new world that may offer new approaches to intractable problems. Iran's Axis of Resistance has suffered catastrophic defeats in Gaza and Lebanon. Tehran's air defenses collapsed in the face of Israeli air strikes. The Islamic Republic has not seemed so vulnerable to foreign attack since the Iran-Iraq War. [91]

First, the United States needs to understand the Middle East's importance to America's national security and our allies. The American people want to abandon the region., and you can't blame them, considering the US spent trillions of dollars in Iraq and Afghan, and lost thousands of lives lost with countless wounded. The results were no better than when we first engaged in combat operations. The Afghan debacle further crystalized to the American public the purpose of us being there in the first place.

Writing for *The Hoover Institution*, in December 2024, Norman Roule perfectly cemented the central reason the Middle East region is "essential to the core of US national security interests and that of our allies."

Stretching from North Africa to the Levant, Iran to the Arabian Sea, the region includes five strategic global chokepoints: the Strait of Gibraltar, the Bosphorus, the Suez Canal, The Bab al-Mandab, and the Strait of Hormuz. A vast percentage of international trade, energy, communications, and transportation pour through these arteries every hour. Depending on its destination, between twenty and thirty percent of global trade moves through these chokepoints. Between seventeen and thirty percent of global internet traffic transits fiber cables in Egypt and the Red Sea. The ambitious India–Middle East–Europe Corridor (IMEC) that would integrate the economies of Europe, the Middle East, and Asia involves multiple regional partners.

The region's religious sites are important to billions of Christians, Jews, and Sunni and Shia Muslims who look to Jerusalem, Mecca, and Najaf daily. Influencing interfaith engagement, counter-extremism, human rights, and counterterrorism cannot be done without the cooperation of regional leaders.

The region's self-generated social and economic transformation will not only reshape its wealthy societies but also provide the investments needed to improve the stability of fragile regional states and overcome the developmental challenges of Africa. The assets managed by the Gulf Cooperation Countries (GCC) sovereign wealth funds exceed a staggering USD four trillion, or more than thirty-seven percent of the global total.

The region is increasingly operating on a global stage. Israel offers world-class technology. The GCC countries are expanding infrastructure investments throughout Africa, Latin America, India, and Asia, competing with China and discouraging corruption. Traditional regional hydrocarbon producers are heavily focused on renewable energy production. The emphasis placed by the United Arab Emirates on COP 28 represented a new focus on a stable transition to greener energies, financial compensation for countries damaged by climate change, and investment in new energy technologies. Gulf leaders have embraced artificial intelligence (AI), as the foundation of their social and economic development for the next century. The AI investments of Saudi Arabia and the United Arab Emirates alone will likely exceed one hundred billion dollars.

Last, Beijing and Moscow also consider the Middle East important for their national interests and welcome opportunities to undercut American influence.[92]

America has committed significant amounts military assets and personnel to contain the various issues in the Middle East. However, President Trump's administration must deal with the ongoing wars in Gaza and Lebanon, as well as fractured allies who feel the United States is abandoning the region. America has committed significant amounts of military assets and personnel to contain the various regional issues. How the US navigates these tumultuous times, considering the weakened Hezbollah in Lebanon, Hamas on the brink of self-destruction, the Syrian regime of Bashar al-Assad collapsed, a weakened Iran, and Russia potentially being extricated from Syria after the regime imploded, will tell how America deals with these crucial developments.

One must factor in US foreign policy and how the global community, allies and adversaries alike, react and view America. Since the end of the Second World War, with the collapse of the Soviet Union and the end of the Cold War, America stood as the dominant superpower and emerged as the only hegemonic power in the world.

In the past, there was no doubt that the US dominated the world in politics, economics, and military strength. This is no longer the case, as other nations have closed the gap. Most concerning is that as China increased its prominence in the world, the US experienced a decline. That doesn't mean Beijing has supplanted the US, but they are nipping at our heels. "Strategic missteps and a shifting global order" contributed to the diminished world view of the US. The result is America's current uphill struggle to reestablish the US as the "indispensable force it once claimed to be."

> One of the clearest signs of the United States' diminishing global influence is that fewer countries are looking to Washington for leadership or guidance in resolving conflicts. This shift became glaringly apparent during the US' chaotic withdrawal from Afghanistan in August 2021. The decision to exit marked a significant strategic failure, not only for its immediate effects, but for the broader ripple it triggered across West Asia and beyond.[93]

Can you blame them? During President Biden's administration, they witnessed America's humiliating withdrawal from Afghanistan, in which we left our allies behind without letting them know of our pulling out so abruptly. During this withdrawal we also left billions of military equipment to the Taliban. The US allowed groups such as al-Qaeda and ISIS-K to regain operation with impunity across the region.

This withdrawal bewildered our allies, but more importantly, it emboldened our adversaries, including Iran, Russia, and China. The US weakened its key alliances in the region like Saudi Arabia, the Gulf States, and Israel.

The Biden Administration's weak and feckless Middle East policy embolden Iran to fund and expand its influence on its proxy forces like Hamas and Hezbollah.

> The decline of US global dominance is further underscored by the rise of China and Russia, two nations that now challenge Washington on multiple fronts. China, with its state-controlled system, has steadily strengthened its political and economic influence, presenting an appealing model for many countries in the developing world. In contrast to the apparent dysfunction

of Western democracies, China's model of governance under President Xi Jinping has garnered interest from nations seeking stability and growth.[94]

The last part and one that Trump advisor Elon Musk and his Department of Government Efficiency (DOGE) task forces his looking at the massive waste fraud and abuse at United States Agency for International Development (USAID). Once the lid was lifted, Americans were stunned to find how billions of dollars were spent that had nothing to do with international development. The purpose of USAID as it was the primary mechanism for administering US foreign aid. USAID is a separate independent agency that reports to the State Department, which bureaucratic infighting always arises over influence and power. USAID needs to be reorganized to impute how foreign aid is administered across the globe that falls inline with US strategic goals set forth by the president. This can be a very effective tool in carrying out an effective US national security strategy. What was uncovered shows how this agency needs a major reorganization and overhaul if it is to meet its core mission.

President Trump has a lot of ground to make up in reassuring our allies that America isn't in decline. To our adversaries, he is sending a profound message: Don't mess with us, the consequences will be devastating for you!

Five

Restoring American Deterrence

Speaking before a Joint Session of both the House and the Senate, President George Washington famously stated in the First Annual Address, to Both Houses of Congress on Friday, January 8, 1790, "To be prepared for war is one of the most effectual means of preserving peace."

After the end of the Cold War, America emerged as a hegemonic power with absolute military, political, and economic capabilities with no near peer competitor to challenge its supremacy. With no rival power to contest its primacy, the US embarked on a strategy of building and reimagining the liberal world order it had established after the Second World War, into a global system where all nations benefited.

Washington pursued a far-ranging global campaign in the wake of the September 11, 2001, terrorist attacks that led it to committing the strategic blunder of invading Iraq and turned a targeted anti–al Qaeda campaign in Afghanistan into a nation-building operation that ultimately failed. It also led to overreach in Europe and set the stage for overreach in Asia.[95]

America's twenty-year legacy of continuous wars throughout the Middle East and Central Asia, coupled with the disastrous withdrawal from Afghanistan, has left an impression of an America in decline. With the United States primarily focused on the Middle East, other nations took advantage. Now, America faces a more multipolar world. With Russia asserting itself in Ukraine, wars in the Middle East, China bolstering its military capabilities in the Indo-Pacific region, and major conflicts ending in both Iraq and Afghanistan, America's military deterrence, to many, is on the decline.

What is the solution? President Trump's Administration faces two choices: Additional military spending or reforming the Department of Defense into meeting its core mission — protecting the homeland and deterring war the better solution.

As of right now, America is not prepared to meet the challenges and threats today, especially if we get into or are forced into a conflict with China. The FY2025 defense budget, which was recently passed, totaled $895.2 billion, but is additional revenue the answer? The Department of Defense has failed the past seven audits. If America is to challenge China and reaffirm America's military deterrence, then its past time to reform the Department of Defense and place it in line with the challenges of a multipolar world.

Since the end of the Cold War, with no competitive power to challenge its primacy, the US re-oriented its defense strategy and focused primarily on lesser regional powers, not on a near peer competitor like China. Like in the 1991 Gulf War, America assumed that it would have months to build its forces to a level to begin combat operations, was safe from attacks on its logistical supply chains, and would have unsurpassed air superiority. This may not be the case in the future.

As America was consumed with the War of Terror throughout the Middle East, China was building up its military capabilities. The US now has an aging military. The last major modernization happened forty years ago under the presidency of President Ronald Reagan. Since the end of the cold War, America has let its defense industrial base erode.

If conflict with China arises, America would be hard pressed to re-supply much needed munitions to the Pacific region, because currently most of our stockpile had been transferred to Ukraine and Israel. Even America's shipbuilding capabilities pale in comparison to China, where one shipyard in China can produce more ships than all of America's shipyards combined. This is not the same situation as when the US was able to arm and supply the world during World War II.

As of the beginning of 2025, the United States was confronted with a naval engineering crisis. China's navy had almost four hundred battle-ready vessels and was projected to continue to build new ships, while US vessels numbered less than three hundred. The challenge for America in keeping up with China's naval growth is that while most of China's naval forces are in the western Pacific, US Naval forces extend to every ocean in the world. In any potential naval conflict with China, it would take considerable time for additional US naval assets to join a fight in the Indo-Pacific region.

> Shipbuilding has been one of the cornerstones of national power ever since the beginning of the Industrial Age, especially after Alfred Thayer Mahan articulated the importance of naval power in his book, "The Influence of Sea Power upon History." Europe took notice and the European powers of the time took notice. The imperial powers of the day measured the balance of power in ships. Industrial inputs such as iron and steel production, port infrastructure, industrial workforce, and technology patents were all closely tied to national power. The United States prevailed in the Second World War and defeated Nazi Germany and Imperial Japan by outbuilding the Axis powers and becoming the world's "arsenal of democracy." Throughout the Cold War, the United States ensured freedom of navigation and transit of the seas. Power projection and offshore balancing remain hallmarks of US strategic primacy made possible by a superior fleet.[96]

One only has to examine the statement made by Fleet Admiral Chester W. Nimitz, USN, on his final day of departure from the Navy department as Chief of Naval Operations in 1948, when he reminded everyone of a remark by Sir Walter Raleigh who declared in the early seventeenth century that "whoever commands the sea, commands the trade; whosoever commands the trade of the world commands the riches of the world, as consequently the world itself." China has been an astute study of history and has examined all the great powers of the past, and the conclusion was all had strong navies to exert their influence. With this in mind China has begun massively leveraging its own commercial and defense base to rival the US.

81

Unfortunately for the United States, we have let our own defense and commercial ship building infrastructure lapse away, currently only one major shipyard is capable of building naval and commercial vessels.[97] In order to create greater workforce synergies China's shipyards are geographically close together to each other,[98] thus it has allowed Beijing to build this commercial shipbuilding capacity into the world's largest navy, at America's expense.

As we discussed in Chapter two, America's educational system doesn't support the skilled crafts needed to work in the naval and commercial shipbuilding industry to produce the number of sea-going vessels need to compete with China. The US needs to understand these would be well-paying union jobs!

> Over the past two decades, Beijing has steadily eroded the US naval position in the Western Pacific. Chinese strategists have effectively pursued an anti-access/area denial strategy to push US forces further away, expanded the People's Liberation Army Navy's reach by constructing artificial maritime features in the South China Sea, and coerced neighboring countries with grey-zone tactics. China did this while the United States was distracted by the War on Terror in the Middle East, which diminished the role of the US Navy in American strategy.[99]

America's naval force has not kept pace with China. Now, Beijing poses the largest navy in the world. The bulk of the Chinese naval force is centered in the Indo-Pacific region, while America must maintain a naval presence all over the globe. This places America at a competitive disadvantage, as it would take some time to move key assets to the Pacific region to back up naval forces already there.

China learned a hard lesson during the Third Taiwan Straight Crisis in 1995-96, in which the US sent two carrier battle groups through the Taiwan Straights, and China was powerless to stop this deployment.[100] This humiliated China, and they vowed to rectify this in the future. China dedicated itself to building up their own navy to challenge the US naval supremacy and to invest in anti-ship missiles to take out US naval aircraft carriers.

Reflecting on this changing power dynamic in the Indo-Pacific region, The Center for Strategic and International Studies conducted 24 different war-game scenarios, with the prime focus being a Chinese amphibious invasion of Taiwan. What was the outcome of their war-gaming study?

> In most scenarios, the United States/Taiwan/Japan defeated a conventional amphibious invasion by China and maintained an autonomous Taiwan. However, this defense came at a high cost. The United States and its allies lost dozens of ships, hundreds of aircraft, and tens of thousands of servicemembers. Taiwan saw its economy devastated. Further, the high losses damaged the US global position for many years. China also lost heavily, and failure to occupy Taiwan might destabilize Chinese Communist Party rule. Victory is therefore, not enough. The United States needs to strengthen deterrence immediately.[101]

The other, more plausible scenario would require a US Naval response to a potential Chinese naval blockade of Taiwan. For military strategists and politicians, such a blockade would create an entirely different, more complicated situation than an amphibious invasion that would leave "US and allied forces with greater capability gaps compared with those revealed for amphibious assault scenario."[102]

Beyond a naval blockade of Taiwan, the Chinese could employ gray zone tactics which would avoid direct military confrontation and employ strategies that utilize competition, coercion, and compliance to achieve Beijing's ultimate objective of subduing the Island without direct military confrontation.

War games only simulated a direct attack on Taiwan, and not a naval blockade of the entirety of Taiwan. This is something military and political leaders need to address and be prepared to prevent this very outcome from becoming reality.

One of the key after-action reports regarding these military exercises was the major deficiency in America's defense industrial base. One can focus on the major internal problems China faces, especially economically. Beijing is now contending with high youth unemployment, a troubled real estate market, massive government debt with many economists stating China has entered a stagflation period. China also must contend with an aging population, diminished birth rates and lower-than expected growth rate. Corruption has also impacted the top level of the Chinese military, with the past three defense ministers and others removed because of corruption.

This all may be true, but the US must recognize how much China's defense industrial base is growing. Despite the country's current economic challenges, its defense spending is soaring, and its defense industry is on a wartime footing. This is far different from America who are operating on a peacetime industrial mode.

> China is rapidly developing and producing weapons systems designed to deter the United States and, if deterrence fails, to emerge victorious in a great-power war. China has already caught up to the United States in its ability to produce weapons at mass and scale. In some areas, China now leads it has become the world's largest shipbuilder by far, with a capacity roughly 230 times as large as that of the United States. Between 2021 and early 2024, China's defense industrial base produced more than 400 modern fighter aircraft and 20 large warships, doubled the country's nuclear warhead inventory and more than doubled its inventory of ballistic and cruise missiles, and developed a new stealth bomber. Over the same period, China increased its number of satellites launches by 50 percent. China now acquires weapons systems at a pace five to six times as fast as the United States. Admiral John Aquilino, the former commander of the US Indo-Pacific Command, has described this military expansion as "the most extensive and rapid buildup since World War II."[103]

In the war game simulation of a conflict in the Taiwanese Strait, this would deplete the US military's inventory of long-range antiship missiles in the first week. It's typical to deplete more ammunition and missiles in a wartime conflict than you would during peacetime military exercise. Any conflict with China would be a heavy naval conflict reminiscent of the major Pacific naval battles of World War II. This is especially true early in the conflict, and Chinese defense would prevent most US aircraft from flying close enough to drop short range munitions.

The shift to renewed great power competition, combined with the globalization of supply chains for many manufactured items, has led to an increased emphasis in US defense planning on "supply chain security, meaning (in this context) awareness and minimization of reliance in US military systems on components, subcomponents, materials, and software from other countries, particularly China and Russia."

The US defense industrial base lacks flexibility and surge capability to make up this and other shortfalls. The United States has an anachronistic contracting and acquisitions system that is much better suited for the leisurely pace of peacetime than for the urgency of wartime. As a 2009 US Department of Defense study bluntly put it, "Major defense programs continue to take ten years or more to deliver less capability than planned, often at two to three times the planned cost." The fragility of defense industry supply chains poses another problem. US defense companies produce limited amounts of key components, such as solid rocket motors, processor assemblies, castings, forgings, ball bearings, microelectronics, and seekers for munitions. Some types of equipment, such as engines and generators, require long lead times. Complicating matters, China dominates the world's advanced battery supply chains and has a monopoly on the global market for several types of raw materials used in the defense sector, such as some iron and ferroalloy metals, nonferrous metals, and industrial minerals. If tensions were to escalate or war to break out, China could cut off US access to these materials and undermine US production of night-vision goggles, tanks, and other defense equipment.[104]

One of the major challenges facing America's defense industrial base is the same thing facing the US manufacturing sector, and that is a shortage of engineers, electricians, pipefitters, shipfitters, and metalworkers. It was recently announced by the US Navy that the first Constellation-class guided missile frigate will be more than a year late due to a shortage of hundreds of workers. This includes welders. This is also the case with various classes of naval vessels Virginia-class fast attack submarines. Even some new guided-missile destroyers which provide key anti-aircraft capabilities to the Navy carrier battle groups are three years behind schedule.

The recently passed defense authorization bill allocates $895.1 billion for the Department of Defense. Does it adequately address America's national security threats? In 2020, the late Anthony Cordesman, military analyst at the Center for Strategic & International Studies, wrote:

> The US has made progress in one area: making increases in the defense

85

budget, but far too many of these increases have gone to funding the readiness and the shopping lists of the US military services. There have been few original ideas and changes that have actually benefitted national security.

The US still lurches from one budget year to the next budget year with no clear path for shaping its strategy, planning, programing, or shift in a direction that goes beyond past underfunding or near-term reactions to events. The US has failed to build effectively on its new National Security Strategy (NSS) issued in 2017. The new strategy was only the rough shell of a real strategy when it was initially issued, and it has never been turned into real plans or any consistent effort at implementation.

The FY2021 budget submission is said to be a strategy-driven document, but it is really a list of each military services' immediate spending priorities with no real strategy for any region, combatant command in key areas, or joint warfare. There is no real future year defense plan, and the only serious planning for the future that has taken place that affects US strategy has come largely out of the combatant commands rather than from the Joint Chiefs of Staff or the Office of the Secretary of Defense.[105]

This lack of strategic thinking hasn't changed since 2020. The US has issued no detailed national security strategy, and this didn't change under the Biden administration. President Joe Biden put forth his administration's national security strategy in 2022, and in some areas, it was better than the first Trump administrations, but in other areas, it followed predictable trends of those laid before. Anthony Cordesman's summary of that document follows.

The document does a good job of describing the administration's broad policy goals in every major area of US strategy and covering the entire globe. It also integrates every major aspect of civil and military policy and focuses on working closely with America's strategic partners, other friendly states, and international institutions.

At the same time, it does not go beyond stating broad goals, and stating how existing policy level initiatives can be strengthened to help achieve them. It does not advance detailed plans, programs, or indications of what new resources will be required. It rarely provides even the most general net assessments of key issues, or details as to what implementation plans exist, as distinguished from stating goals for existing initiatives.

In broad terms, it still has all too many of the defects of the Trump national strategy; it may identify China, and Russia as the major threats, but it does not assess their current civil and military capabilities, and ongoing force developments. It does not compare their rates of civil and military change with the rates in the US and its major strategic partners. It tacitly assumes most current US plans and budgets are adequate and that the cooperative efforts with America's strategic partners will achieve the level of common effectiveness and interoperability necessary to compensate for years of force cuts and underinvestment in every aspect of the military capability of most NATO countries.[106]

The strategy put forth is too vague with not enough "meat on the bones" to produce an effective, comprehensive, detailed national security strategy. It leaves out realistic priorities of action. It does not give detailed threat assessments of our adversaries, namely Russia and China, in more detail, nor the vulnerabilities and strengths of US capabilities and our strategic partners.

The national security strategy barely highlights US strategic partnerships and international cooperation with our allies across the globe and does not address costs or current plans. Very little was mentioned of plans, programs, or budget recommendations for future defense budgets. The national security strategy assumes the current policies and budget requests are adequate for the current threats the US faces. Finally, very little is mentioned of specific defense programs now or in the future.

It is time for the United States to recast the basic defense strategy that has been in place since the end of the Cold War. That strategy, which we characterize as decisive expeditionary force, held that, when confronted with a major aggressor somewhere in the world threatening US interests, the United States would marshal overwhelming conventional force; project that power to the region and, perhaps, the homeland of the enemy; and impose its will on that country, producing decisive victory. The strategy was predicated on US military forces that were superior in all domains to those of any adversary. That superiority is gone, surely with respect to China but in significant ways with respect to the forces of other, less powerful adversaries as well, and it is not coming back. At its root, the problem is that the United

States and its allies no longer have a virtual monopoly on the technologies and capabilities that made them so dominant against the forces of nations like Iraq, Serbia, and Afghanistan—near-real-time sensing, high-capacity communications links, precision guidance via miniaturized electronics, and advanced software being primary among these.[107]

The other challenge the US faces is that the defense budget process is badly broken and needs major reform if we are going to address the challenges confronting the US in a multipolar world.

The US defense budgeting process is flawed and ineffective. It takes an immense amount of time to program each dollar we spend, and once allocated, funds must be spent as indicated, even if plans or needs change. Expenditures are based on the fragmented and burdensome decisions made in Congress, not on input from Department of Defense (DOD) leaders. "Today's defense budget contains approximately three thousand line-item appropriations (or silos) where money must be spent and where money may not be moved."[108]

The other area in the defense budget process is one that plagues all government agencies, and that is "use it or lose it" spending practice. This is where you have unused funds, and you are forced to spend it. If you don't, then the chance is that it will be seen as your agency, or in this case the Department of Defense did not need this amount. In the next budget cycle you will be punished with loss of revenue.

The defense budget is burdened with a significant and increasing number of programs and activities that do not produce military capability. Absent intervention, this trend is likely to continue. In addition, the defense budget is not structured to answer today's important management and oversight questions or to meet requirements at a speed of relevance for a modern ready force. The current budget structure does not easily tell us what we are spending on military capability and does not enable quickly producing and fielding the force we require.[109]

The Department of Defense needs to get back to its core mission of defending the homeland and deterring war. Anything that deviates from this mission harms America's national security. Currently, the US spends over $100 billion on non-defense related areas. This revenue could be better allocated for more key naval vessels, much needed mutations, additional attack-submarines, and additional weapons systems across the defense force.

The term *national security* is used too broadly and needs to focus on the core strategy, not morphed into non-defense related missions. American history is littered with examples of presidents from both parties who have spoken about reforming the Pentagon, with former Secretary of Defense Robert Gates laminating his biggest regret of not being able to reform the massive Pentagon bureaucracy.

In his final days, President Eisenhower gave his famous farewell address urging the nation to "guard against the acquisition of unwarranted influence, whether sought or unsought, by the military-industrial complex. The potential for the disastrous rise of misplaced power exists and will persist." In the proceeding decades the US has consistently failed to address the antiquated procurement and acquisition of the Pentagon budgetary system.

Historians often reference the iconic term Eisenhower used referring to the "military industrial complex" which has become famous, but one must look back at the original draft to find what he originally wanted to include was the "Congressional military industrial complex," but elected officials deemed that combination to be too inflammatory.

Eisenhower was referencing military leaders who always seek the latest weapons program without contemplating future threats to the United States. Anthony Cordesman of the Center for Strategic & International Studies also cautions defense leaders who base their budget decisions on what's best for their branch of service instead of tying requests to the current national security strategy.[110]

Far too often, missing in this debate is how political leaders use the Pentagon as a job creation program for their states or districts. Democrats often want a leaner Defense department and want weapons systems reduced, except when it falls it targets their state or district.

Over the decades, the Pentagon has cancelled various weapons programs because of advent failures. In 2013, Lieutenant Colonel Daniel Davis penned an article in *Armed Forces Journal*, "Purge the Generals," focused precisely on this.

Mentioned in the article are few Pentagon weapons failures:

1. The RAH-66 Comanche armed reconnaissance helicopter (launched in 1991 and canceled after $6. 9 billion spent)
2. The XM2001 Crusader mobile cannon (launched in 1995 and canceled after $7 billion spent)
3. The Future Combat Systems (launched in 2003 and canceled after $20 billion spent)[111]

This systematic problem of weapons failures at that Pentagon was not just confined just to the Army; each military branch continues to face this problem of expending resources and failing to deliver the desired results.

The Marine Corps, by order of the Defense Department in 2011, cancelled the Marine Corps' expeditionary fighting vehicle after spending $3 billion. The Navy's Littoral Combat Ship, which was designed to protect coastal regions, has had a slew of cost overruns.

After 16 years and costing $30 billion with each ship costing 250% more than was originally proposed, even after becoming operational a decade ago the ships have experience numerous technical issues that the Department of the Navy doesn't deem them ready for service in the Gulf which was its primary mission.

The public needs to understand how utterly broken the Department of Defense procurement and acquisition system is, just check out Lockheed Martin Corp.'s F-35 jet, the costliest fighter ever with a production cost of over $1.5 Trillion over its 55-year lifespan. This cost keeps rising!

Far too often, blame is placed on the Pentagon who always want the next new weapons system, but equal share must be shared with politicians of both political parties for the bloated defense budget.

In 2013, then-Army Chief of Staff Gen. Ray Odierno testified before Congress, stating the Army had no use for additional M-1 Abrams tanks. Against Odierno's request Congress approved $436 million for the construction and maintenance of Abrams tanks, if appropriated correctly would have gone to more pressing defense needs.

Unfortunately for the US and the Army, only one area of the country produces the tank and that is at the Army Tank Plant in Lima, Ohio, with Lawmakers from both political parties Ohio lawmakers, such as then Democratic Senator Sherrod Brown and Republican Senator Rob Portman, as well as from Republican Representative Jim Jordan.

Again, what politicians want is to eliminate jobs in a crucial swing state like Ohio and lose 16,000 jobs. Congress always seem to state that this is protecting national security, and this is not the only example. The list abounds of this type of appropriation by Congress. Two examples of this are:

Since 2015, the Navy has spent about $3.7 billion modernizing seven of the *Ticonderoga* class guided-missile cruisers—large surface combatants that provide key air defense capabilities. However, only three of the seven ships will complete modernization, and none will gain 5 years of service life, as intended. The Navy wasted $1.84 billion modernizing four cruisers that have now been divested prior to deploying. The Navy also experienced contractor performance and quality issues across the cruiser effort. For example, the contractor performed poor quality work on USS Vicksburg's sonar dome—a critical element of the Anti-Submarine Warfare mission area—resulting in additional cost and schedule delays due to necessary rework.[112]

In the two years since America's National Defense Strategy heralded the return of great power competition, military leaders have called for US forces to rapidly adopt new technologies ranging from hypersonic missiles and directed energy weapons to artificial intelligence and autonomous vehicles. Outside of special operations, however, the Pentagon's post-Cold War track record of fielding cutting-edge gear is, at best, uneven. The Army future combat system, Navy's Ford-class aircraft carrier, and the Air Force KC-46 Tanker are just a few recent examples where technological hurdles slowed or stopped introduction of a new program service leaders considered essential to stay ahead of adversaries.[113]

These issues are compounded by congressional input that lacks consideration or understanding of the military's needs. Members of Congress have traditionally procured supplies from their constituents in order to satisfy their communities and create jobs at home. This leaves the military saddled with stocks of items and equipment that it does not need or want. Consequently, the Pentagon is obligated to use outdated or useless contracts and programs. The same goes for personnel. Delayed retirements and other efforts to keep the number of troops at a maximum are well-meaning, but these actions negatively affect future spending and technological advancement.

> By establishing gates and milestones for DoD to meet before starting a new program, Congress should gain the confidence to support service technology investments and stop the practice of marking R&D spending that seems "orphaned" or ahead of need. Members will also need to reduce the urge to create more sustainment bills for DoD by buying additional ships and aircraft or unnecessarily retaining those already in service.

> The Pentagon can do a better job for its part by using more realistic operational and fiscal assumptions to guide future force requirements, as well as clearly defining the path to maturing the technologies necessary to realize its vision. When future defense plans are developed, services need to better communicate the details with Congress and other stakeholders.

> Unless Congress and DoD can work together as a team, the dysfunction common to many new defense programs will continue. Today's once-in-a-century combination of a pandemic, intensifying great power competition, and looming fiscal challenges creates an imperative for the US military to become more capable and affordable. Congressional and Pentagon leaders need to reach across the Potomac or risk US forces becoming unsustainable and uncompetitive.[114]

To return the Department of Defense to regain American deterrence, even before beginning his second term, President Trump considered drafting an executive order which would establish a "warrior board" staffed by senior military personnel who would have the power to review all three-four-star officers and make recommendations on who should be removed as unfit to serve in combat commands. Many have cited this would upend the military review process and be seen as politicization of the military.

The Biden administration threw the Pentagon into the political woke agenda movement. In the "most extreme politicization of US military forces in modern history," everything from "the abortion debate, to mandating force-wide diversity, equity, inclusion simars, to promoting climate activism . . . to quixotic campaigns to weed out domestic extremists," hindered military readiness, recruiting, and preparation for combat.[115]

In his first term, Trump had a tumultuous relationship with his then Secretary of Defense James Mattis since he was invited to the Tank, located in the Pentagon's outer circle. By bringing Trump to the Pentagon, they thought he would be swayed by the pageantry and history of the institution and come to see their way of thinking on Afghanistan. Instead, they received something far different, as Trump erupted over what was presented as a strategy on Afghanistan — after close to twenty years of conflict in the country. Trump's calculation is all about winning, and in his estimation, America has not won a war since World War II, despite trillions spent and thousands of American casualties with no positive outcome for the US.

American history is full of examples of American presidents removing military commanders. The act of removing bad or distracted leaders is a tool as old as war itself.

> President Lincoln went through several field commanders before settling on Ulysses S. Grant. Patton took over for Lloyd Fredenhall, whose failure at the Kasserine Pass in North Africa resulted in a catastrophic American defeat. President Eisenhower replaced General Matthew Ridgway with Maxwell Taylor after a policy disagreement over military end-strength. Barack Obama purportedly found Marine general James Mattis too aggressive for leadership of the US Central Command and fired him, an act all but celebrated by Manhattan editors and DC think tanks.[116]

> Upon taking office in 1939, with Franklin Roosevelt's support and authority, Marshall began creating a new army, purging from it more than a thousand officers he deemed unfit and reshaping the standard Army division by transforming its four large but undermanned regiments into three smaller

and more effective regiments with full manpower and greater mobility. Men whose names would become famous in the war in Europe would emerge as stars during the training of the draftees in the 1941 maneuvers. Atop the list was the brilliant but arrogant George S. Patton, a veteran of the First World War.[117]

The issue raised by Trump wasn't the first time this crisis in our military hierarchy was raised. Almost twenty years ago, Lt. Col. Paul Yingling wrote an article in *Armed Forces Journal*, titled "A Failure in Generalship." Lt. Col. Yingling was responding to the then ongoing insurgency America was fighting inside Iraq.

These debacles are not attributable to individual failures, but rather to a crisis in an entire institution: America's general officer corps. America's generals have failed to prepare our armed forces for war and advise civilian authorities on the application of force to achieve the aims of policy. The argument that follows consists of three elements. First, generals have a responsibility to society to provide policymakers with a correct estimate of strategic probabilities. Second, America's generals in Vietnam and Iraq failed to perform this responsibility. Third, remedying the crisis in American generalship requires the intervention of Congress.

To prevail, generals must provide policymakers and the public with a correct estimation of strategic probabilities. The general is responsible for estimating the likelihood of success in applying force to achieve the aims of policy. The general describes both the means necessary for the successful prosecution of war and the ways in which the nation will employ those means. If the policymaker desires end for which the means he provides are insufficient, the general is responsible for advising the statesman of this incongruence. The statesman must then scale back the ends of policy or mobilize popular passions to provide greater means. If the general remains silent while the statesman commits a nation to war with insufficient means, he shares culpability for the results.

America's generals have repeated the mistakes of Vietnam in Iraq. First, throughout the 1990s our generals failed to envision the conditions of future combat and prepare their forces accordingly. Second, America's generals failed to estimate correctly both the means and the ways necessary to achieve the aims of policy prior to beginning the war in Iraq. Finally, America's generals did not provide Congress and the public with an accurate assessment of the conflict in Iraq.[118]

Missing in educational development, the US military needs to take a page from history and study how General Fox Conner, who served as the operations officer of the American Expeditionary Force (AEF) under General John "Blackjack" Pershing in World War I. Conner would mentor upcoming officers, including future generals such as George Marshall, Geoge Patton, and especially Dwight Eisenhower.

After the war, Connor took a command position at the Panama Canal. Major George Patton, whom he had met years before on a train, recommended Major Dwight Eisenhower as his executive officer.

There was only one problem. Ike was facing a court-martial over a $250 housing allowance he'd claimed for his son who was living with his wife's parents. It was a mistake, and Eisenhower tried to correct it. But the gears of Army bureaucracy were all but inexorable. It took the personal and persistent ministrations of Conner through George Marshall to quash the proceedings and allow Ike's transfer to go through.

Three years of focused company in Panama with the cerebral Fox Conner elevated the unsophisticated Major Eisenhower into something larger. Conner had brought a library of books with him and began assigning volumes to his protégé, then reviewing them with the Socratic method. "And thus began a three-year graduate school course in military affairs and humanities," Ike would later recall. Conner also worked on Eisenhower's rigid and overbearing demeanor with troops and encouraged the more familiar, casual but highly disciplined style we know from World War Two.

In Panama, Conner warned Eisenhower to prepare himself for another World War, which he said was "almost a certainty." He predicted George Marshall, whom Conner called "nothing short of a genius," would play a key role, and he told Ike to study applied psychology so he could learn to "get allies of different nations to march and think as a nation."[119]

Conner then introduced Eisenhower to Clausewitz. Eisenhower struggled to grasp the maxims set forth by Clausewitz, so Conner had Eisenhower read the book three times. Conner would quiz Eisenhower as to what each Clausewitzian principle meant. In a 1966 letter, Eisenhower identified *On War* as the book that had most profoundly influenced his military career. Patton recounted one World War II debate over strategy in which Eisenhower became "very pontifical and quoted Clausewitz to us."

Eisenhower continued to explore Conner's military library. He analyzed, and re-fought on paper, the campaigns of Napoleon and of Frederick the Great of Prussia. Having read Churchill's fictional accounts of Ulysses S. Grant and William T. Sherman in *The Crisis*, Eisenhower read the memoirs of both generals. Additionally, Eisenhower read the leading scholarly works of the time on the Civil War, including those of Matthew Forney Steele. Eisenhower then studied the recently fought World War. Conner and Eisenhower "war gamed" the battles of World War I to analyze mistakes made by the war's commanders. They debated the effectiveness of the delaying actions of Lee at the end of the Civil War and of Ludendorff at the conclusion of the Great War. Conner thought Ludendorff's strategy had been superior.

Conner focused Eisenhower's attention on the decisions—good and bad—that history's great commanders had made. Why was a particular decision made? Under what conditions? What were the alternatives? How might a different decision have affected the outcome?

The two discussed what Eisenhower termed "the long history of man, his ideas, and works." In their discussions, Conner sometimes quoted from Shakespeare, to relate passages from the bard's plays of kings and conquests in earlier centuries to more contemporary conflicts and characters. Conner told Eisenhower: "In all military history, only one thing never changes—human nature. Terrain may change, weather may change, weapons may change...but never human nature." Not surprisingly, Conner also introduced Eisenhower to the works of Plato and other philosophers, including Nietzsche.

In his lessons to Eisenhower, Conner stressed important lessons of modern warfare: 1). Never fight unless you have to; 2). Never fight alone; and 3). Never fight for long. Eisenhower frequently thereafter used two particular sayings he had learned from Conner: "Always take your job seriously, never yourself;" and "All generalities are false, including this one."

Connor brought up a topic that would have prophetic applications for the future.

Conner explained to Eisenhower that any future allied commander would face the same resistance Marshal Foch had encountered during the Great War—such as Conner's own strong opposition to amalgamation of American soldiers—when attempting to control troops of a foreign nation. Conner stressed the need for allied nations to develop a command structure that vested the supreme commander with stronger powers than Foch had held. Conner thought that the general atop the international coalition would need to be as much a boardroom conciliator as a battlefield commander. Therefore, Conner stressed the need for a future supreme commander to be skilled in the "art of persuasion." Eisenhower recalled that Conner would "get out a book of applied psychology and we would talk it over...How do you get allies of different nations to march and think as a nation?"[120]

This sort of mentorship is what's missing in our military hierarchy today. We have the various war colleges, but nothing like this type of mentorship of junior officers who will one day be the future generals and admirals leading America's armed forces and giving advice on the conduct of the principle articulated by Clausewitz to national leaders.

Six

America's Eyes and Ears

Over ten years ago, former Army Chief of Staff Gen. Raymond Odierno, former Marine Corps Commandant Gen. James Amos, and former Commander of US Special Operations Command Adm. William McRaven observed that "conflict and competition are about people." As a result "influencing these people—be they heads of state, tribal elders, and militaries and their leaders, or even an entire population"—remains essential to securing US interests.[121]

America has forgotten this aspect, and far too long the United States places greater importance on intelligence gathering, which comes from imagery, open-source, signals, geospatial, but fails to truly develop the human intelligence gathering capabilities into its intelligence gathering. Often without a truly comprehensive human intelligence (HUMINT), mistakes are made, and strategic national security strategies are badly put forth.

This was never more evident than in the conflicts the US found itself engaged in Iraq and Afghanistan. Once the United States initiated combat operations inside Afghanistan following the September 11, 2001, terror attacks on the US homeland, the US repeated the very mistakes made by other empires in trying to subdue the Afghan population. Each empire repeated the very mistakes made by the last empire by failing to understand the history and tribal dynamics of the country. Once America began combat operations in the fall of 2001, the US had no understanding of the country, didn't have anyone who could speak the different tribal dialects, and had no one who understood the Afghan people or tribal nuances.

One of the key mistakes made by the US transpired a decade before the September 11 terror attack on the US homeland, when the last Russian soldier left Afghanistan. Once this happened, America virtually abandoned the country. The US withdrawal left a void without any human intelligence gathering being conducted. This lack of crucial information would be the Achilles heel for the US when combat operations began shortly after September 11.

This failure of human intelligence of the region led to some of the most disastrous decisions, which had consequential strategic national security outcomes not only in the Middle East/Central Asian region, but across the globe.

For the US to have a fully capable intelligence apparatus, it needs to understand how human geography impacts intelligence gathering. First and foremost, the US has to understand that the world around us does not follow the parameters set forth in western thought, norms, or political theory. Far too often, US national security leaders, especially US political leaders, look at the global landscape through rose-colored glasses, expecting every government and political system to look just like our own. This is impossible to replicate, because many people do not want our system or customs.

Human geography is essential to understanding the potential of people. It "reveals what people look like, what they think, and how they behave. It enables one to interpret human behaviors and attitudes over space and time, as well as delineate physical, political, and cultural borders."[122] Militarily, it is a vital component of national security policy that enables decision-makers to "get ahead of the curve to protect US interests at home and abroad." Knowledge of the population's ideology in a specific region imparts a military advantage and creates an understanding of "whether a population has the will to fight or how a partner country's geopolitical allegiances may be shifting." Understanding the human component is a better practice than past methods of data collection, which proved ineffective and did not account for "an increasingly complex, contested, and chaotic world."[123]

Two vital scenarios played out. First, the US was blindsided and left stunned when, in mid-2021, the United States pulled out of Afghanistan. The Afghan government rapidly collapsed in the face of the Taliban withdrawal, and US military forces exited the country. Second, US intelligence leaders grossly underestimated the willingness and the ability of Ukraine to defend itself against the Russian onslaught. The other failure of intelligence was the sudden pivot by Niger after a coup in July of 2023. This forced the US to withdraw its military and diplomatic forces from that country and then welcome Russia to replace America.

> In Afghanistan, for example, the international community spent millions of dollars at the capital-city level in Kabul building a Supreme Court and training judges and rewriting the legal code and so on, to establish a rule-of-law system. The Taliban came in at the village level with Sharia and their mobile courts, and they established a rule-of-law system within months and gained control of the population while we were still busy turning around in Kabul. So one of the other lessons we've drawn from this is that bottom-up, community-based law, which can be transitional justice, or customary law, applied by traditional courts or religious courts, is as effective and possibly even more effective in the initial stages than central-state structures; particularly in a place like Afghanistan or some parts of South Asia and Africa where there isn't a strong tradition of central-state presence anyway.[124]

In a turbulent world, the capacity for America to report accurate information through Human Intelligence is ineffective or missing. Far too often, we examine things through the lens of how we see them and what we would do in certain situations. Unfortunately, the world does not operate like that. "This lack of human eyes and ears in areas of the world critical to our national security and economic interests has led to poor decision making." The ineffectiveness of Human Intelligence contributed to our inability to anticipate and prepare for events. Being reactive instead of proactive resulted in catastrophic consequences, such as the attack on 9/11, the wars in the Middle East, and the continued injuries and loss of lives throughout US forces.[125]

Human Intelligence is the collection of information from human sources. The collection may be done openly, as when FBI agents interview witnesses or suspects, or it may be done through clandestine or covert means (espionage). Within the United States, HUMINT collection is the FBI's responsibility. Beyond US borders, HUMINT is generally collected by the CIA, but also by other US components abroad.[126]

US national security leaders need to understand the capability and the importance of HUMIT, not only on the battlefield, but when making policy decisions. It is important for the US to comprehend the mind of the opposing leader we are dealing with. Following the Iraq war, a detailed report by the Senate Committee on Intelligence concluded that there were "significant shortcomings in almost every aspect of the Intelligence Community's human intelligence collection efforts against Iraq's weapons of mass destruction activities." This critical strategic intelligence deficit was created in 1998, when "UN inspectors were forced out of the country." America lost its eyes and ears on what was happening on the ground and was not able to collect real-world, real-time intelligence. This left the intelligence community with no capability of gathering information in Iraq. Corrupt business dealings and inept leadership exasperated the issue. Therefore, such intelligence failures cannot be resolved with increased funds or more workers.[127]

The problem listed by the Senate Committee was that the Intelligence Community relied far too much on United Nations (UN) inspectors for much of the intel on Iraq's nuclear program without sufficient utilization of HUMINT collection from individuals with more robust knowledge of the program. The United States lacked sufficient human presence inside the Iraq to gain valuable insight into how far or to what aspect the nuclear program was progressing or is progressing.

The difficulty for the United States is that America has almost no human assets in countries hostile to the US, such as Iran, Russia, China, and North Korea, and even countries technically friendly to the US as Saudi Arabia and others. The US does not have skilled people trained in the languages, intelligence operations, and especially the cultural and historical knowledge of the country assigned. The US has not done a great enough job of employing individuals from these countries to report on their country of origin.

Utilizing individuals is essential, as these people know the various cultural nuances, which only a native-born person would pick up. No matter how much scholastic education one has it still does not replicate the knowledge of being born into the culture. America seems to rely far too much on high technology for its intelligence gathering capabilities at the expense of relegating HUMINT to second tier status in the intelligence community.

If you use Israel as an example, they utilize the *Mista'arvim*, "an elite Israeli undercover unit whose operatives disguise themselves as Palestinians or Arabs to gather intelligence, infiltrate protests, and carry out assassinations."[128]

On October 1, 2024, the *Times of Israel* reported that an Israeli double agent had infiltrated Iran's secret service and become the head of one of their units targeting Mossad agents. The double agent was in the perfect position to supply Israel with details of Iran's nuclear capabilities.[129]

I am not suggesting that we duplicate every aspect of Israel's unit, but if America had better human intelligence capabilities inside many of the countries which are hostile to the US, we could have a variety of different options for national leaders instead of going blindly into a situation with faulty or non-existent intelligence of a given country or region.

After the Cold War, the US all but eliminated the use of HUMINT in favor of more technologically advanced options. Military and civilian leaders touted electronic intelligence systems as the epitome of information acquisition. Beginning with airborne electronic surveillance in Vietnam, at first as a supplement to undercover spies, then eventually as a convenient replacement for HUMINT intelligence, the new technology was regarded as a perfect modern replacement for the usual, old-fashioned spy techniques.

> Since that time, the US has spent the vast majority of its intelligence related military research and development funds on sophisticated technology, especially in the area of signals intelligence (SIGNET). SIGNET and electronic intelligence (ELINT) is used by both satellites and drones to locate and then intercept transmissions from sources such as cell phones, radio, television,

weapons systems, and the Internet. It is extremely effective in all of those tasks. What SIGNET cannot capture or analyze however, is the human mind.[130]

Many could point to the targeted killing of Iranian Islamic Revolutionary Guard Corps (IRGC) Commander General Qasem Soleimani was successful because of America's highly sophisticated signal intelligence capabilities. The limitations were, yes, we killed Soleimani, but we were unable gauge the reaction nor could we predict how Tehran would act, since the US had no reliable assets on the ground inside Iran. This targeted strike proved successful, but many others were not. Just look back at the targeted strike in Afghanistan on August 29, 2021, that killed 10 civilians, to include seven children.

Then Commanding General of United States Central Command, General Kenneth F. McKenzie Jr. commented at a Pentagon press briefing that we did not have proper actionable intelligence on the ground but relied solely on aerial reconnaissance in making our decision the launch the air strike.[131] In this case, a viable HUMIT capability may or may not have prevented this missile strike, but having human intelligence on the ground would have possibly helped to achieve better outcomes.

The lack of credible HUMINT assets in China failed to provide the United States accurate or timely information on the start and then spread of the coronavirus in Huanan ... Although we had some reports starting late in December 2019 of the mounting health crisis in China from secondary sources, the US did not have any reliable American controlled agents in Huanan that could have provided Intelligence and health officials in Washington with accurate information back in December 2019 or even in January 2020, early enough to have prevented the spread of the virus to millions of Americans. That short, early window for the flow of crucial information from reliable HUMINT sources on the ground in China in December 2019 could have possibly prevented the catastrophic pandemic that inevitably followed in the United States, an intelligence failure so massive that it will possibly be remembered as a worse tragedy than the intelligence failure just before 9/11.[132]

HUMINT has two different applications — one at the tactical level for military commanders to better understand the battle space they will be operating in, and the other for political leaders dealing with foreign leaders and the countries they lead.

The military calls this counterinsurgency (COIN), as the center of gravity is the civilian population. This was lost on US national security planners as they began the planning phase for the invasion of Iraq. Without re-litigating the Iraq war, former United States Central Command (CENTCOM), led by Marine General Anthony Zinni (ret.), put forth a series of war-games known as Desert Crossing in order to assess the feasibility if the government of Saddam Hussein fell from an internal uprising or forcibly removed by the United States and its allies.

> The results of Desert Crossing, however, drew pessimistic conclusions regarding the immediate possible outcomes of such action. Some of these conclusions are interestingly similar to the events which actually occurred after Saddam was overthrown. The report forewarned that regime change may cause regional instability by opening the doors to "rival forces bidding for power" which, in turn, could cause societal "fragmentation along religious and/or ethnic lines" and antagonize "aggressive neighbors." Further, the report illuminated worries that secure borders and a restoration of civil order may not be enough to stabilize Iraq if the replacement government were perceived as weak, subservient to outside powers, or out of touch with other regional governments. An exit strategy, the report said, would also be complicated by differing visions for a post-Saddam Iraq among those involved in the conflict.[133]

One of the major deficiencies of Iraqi Freedom was over-confidence in our assumptions, but without effective HUMINT capabilities inside Iraq, we never got a sense of the mood of the Iraqi people, nor did we understand the tribal and religious factions inside the country. Proper HUMINT capabilities would have let US planners know how the Iraqi people felt about the Iraqi army verse the much-hated vaunted Republican Guard military forces whose loyalty ran strictly to the ruling government of Saddam Hussain.

As Operation Iraqi Freedom began, it became evident that US HUMIT did not understand, nor were they prepared for the situation. As soldiers became more familiar with the populations, they began to realize that the insurgents were embedded with civilians. The only way to succeed in these military operations was to gain insight into the people of the region and interact with them in such a way as to attain their trust and cooperation.

Anyone who studies counterinsurgency will agree that the insurgents have several advantages. They are fluent in the language, know the local customs and interests, and comprehend the political climate of the region. They usually do not wear uniforms, making it difficult to differentiate them from innocent civilians. Unfortunately, national security strategists and policymakers more often than not exude an arrogance that they know what's best simply because of their education or status. The greatest failure of US endeavors in the Middle East was failing to listen to those closest to the ground who could have told them their strategy was flawed.[134]

The main problem is that little information was available on the tribal and religious faction inside both Iraq and Afghanistan before combat operations began. After the terror attack on September 11, 2001, the US military ramped up rapidly to confront the threat it was going to face, but just from an open-source perspective. Little detailed knowledge was available. If information was presented, it was compiled from a western perspective and not how the people of the region viewed things.

To get a better understanding how to have a viable HUMINT intelligence perspective, the US needs to examine the origins of the Operation of Strategic Service (OSS) run by William Joseph "Wild Bill" Donovan, who also is the father of the Central Intelligence Agency formed after World War II as part of the National Security Act of 1947.

One first must understand who Donovan was and how he built the OSS during World War II, and how he was a voracious reader of politics and economics, but especially the world around him. He traveled extensively and in his travels in the inter-war years meet he met with various world leaders, some before they gained prominence in World War II, such as his early meeting in the late 1920s with Adolf Hitler. Donovan believed it was essential to meet with people, not just leaders of a country, but ordinary individuals who could provide local incites.

In the 1920s, Donovan traveled to Europe visiting the various capitals of Europe and by mingling with the local population, got a real since of what life was like for ordinary people. In his travels he corresponded with European business leaders who had extensive knowledge of economics and business.

Donovan was an early student of HUMINT. Instead of looking at items from a corporate perspective, he traveled and viewed them firsthand. For example, he saw the factories and industrial plants to observe concrete details. This imminent detail had Donovan observing the Japanese in Manchuria and obtaining permission from the Italian Dictator Benito Mussolini to observe Italian forces invitation of Ethiopia to get a sense of their military capabilities and prowess. The purpose was to get a sense of the Italian armies' military capabilities. Were they the same army that fought in World War I?

Donovan would write, "During the 1930s, as a private citizen I visited Ethiopia, Spain, and other European countries to see what modern war would mean. All other nations, even little ones, had capable secret intelligence agencies. We had only the conventional intelligence service of the Department of State, with its military and naval attaches, and the agencies attached to the War and Navy Departments, which limited themselves narrowly to items of purely military information."

With war on the horizon, Donovan became increasingly concerned by the buildup of Italian military power in Eritrea. He knew from his friend, Italian Ambassador Augusto Rossi, that Italy's dictator was determined to conquer a new market for Italian exports and solve Italy's crucial unemployment problem. To avoid a previous defeat at Aduwa in 1896, and to prove to the world Fascism would be victorious in battle, Donovan returned to America, convinced of Italy's planned invasion of Ethiopia no matter the League of Nations would do.[135]

> Once Donovan began to staff the OSS, he brought in anyone and everyone who could be useful in intelligence gathering. First, Donovan sent his intelligence operators to the New York library system to learn everything about the area and regions in which they would be operating. Donovan wanted to know every intricate detail of a given area.
>
> With a free hand in hiring, Donovan began by enlisting a number of his

able associates and then began recruiting Americans who had traveled abroad or were otherwise well versed in world affairs. In the early 1940s, that often meant educated or affluent members of the American elites or foreign émigrés. Donovan relied upon his personal contacts with people he or his subordinates trusted, and he drew most of his top aides from prestigious colleges and universities, businesses, and law firms, including his own. As the war approached and particularly after the United States entered the war following the Pearl Harbor attack in December 1941, many Americans volunteered to serve their country. In that rush to service, Donovan's COI and its successor, the OSS, drew such a disproportionate number of socially prominent men and women that some wags claimed the initials of O. S. S. stood for "Oh-So-Social." Although prominent people held a number of high-level positions in the agency, the vast majority of the men and women recruited by the OSS were neither prominent nor listed in the Social Register. First priorities were to obtain experts to evaluate incoming intelligence and also propagandists who would use some of that research to undermine enemy morale abroad. As early as June 1941, Donovan had obtained the support of the Librarian of Congress, poet Archibald MacLeish, to allow the prospective organization to use the library's extensive materials in analyzing the Axis' strengths and weaknesses. In July, Donovan hired the President of Williams College, James Phinney Baxter III, a historian, to head the COI's Research and Analysis (R&A) Branch. Baxter and Donovan quickly recruited noted scholars in various disciplines from prestigious colleges and universities and put them to work in the Library of Congress Among the early recruits were Harvard historian William L. Langer; Edward Meade Earle from the Institute for Advanced Study in Princeton; economist Edward S. Mason from Harvard; Joseph Hayden, a University of Michigan political scientist and former vice governor of the Philippines; historian Sherman Kent of Yale; Wilmarth S. Lewis, millionaire Yale biographer of Horace Walpole; and James L. McConaghy, President of Wesleyan University, and many others. Within a few months, Donovan began sending to Roosevelt summaries of detailed R&A reports on strategic economic, political, social, and military information about conditions and strategic prospects in Europe, North Africa, and the Middle East. Robert E. Sherwood, noted playwright, pacifist turned interventionist and a speech writer for the President, enthusiastically endorsed the idea of undermining enemy morale and bolstering resistance via short-wave radio broadcasts and other media aimed at Nazi Germany and

German-occupied countries, and Donovan quickly chose him to head COI's Foreign Information Service. Within a few months, Donovan added a Visual Presentation Branch, which would include Hollywood directors John Ford, famous for his westerns and other epics, and Merian C. Cooper, adventurer/ filmmaker and creator of King Kong. To facilitate COI's work in Europe and the German-occupied countries there, Donovan, with the permission of Roosevelt and Churchill, set up an office in London in October 1941, the first of many overseas regional headquarters.[136]

As in Donovan's era, with all the conflicts erupting across the globe, US military advisors should be observing the conflict in Ukraine and viewing how Ukrainian and forces operate, but also the morale of the forces engaged, which means speaking with enlisted troops and civilians. Are we observing the operation of these military forces in real time?

Are we getting a first-hand examination of how the Russian military operates in a war-time environment and their operating capabilities?

Have defense experts visited the border region between India and China in the Ladakh area to fully understand how both the Indian and Chinese armies fight? Have US senior military officials spent time with the Indian military in asking how they dealt with the Chinese military over the decades?

The same could be said of US military officials speaking with Vietnamese defense officials who are still around from the 1979 Sino-Vietnamese War and getting their perspective and the lessons learned from that conflict, especially how China conducts warfare.

Far too often, US policy leaders have a distorted knowledge of foreign leaders they are dealing with, and this includes Russian President Vladimir Putin. Each US president who has had to deal with Putin believes they understand him and what his ultimate gain is, but each has also looked at the Russian leader though a warped view of western global thought process.

Does the United States even understand Russia and how they view the world around them? Russia has always been in a state of turmoil, as it fluctuates between east and west. The west associate's expansion with wealth and power, were Russia views expansion with poverty and insecurity. Far too often, US presidents have failed to understand

Putin. They need to realize he is a fervent nationalist, who looks to the past and tries to replicate Russian greatness and reestablish the old Russian empire. To Putin, Ukraine, Crimea and the Central Asian republics are always synonymous with Russia.[137]

Like all the Russian leaders before him, Putin's outlook is shaped by the past. Putin intertwines his political behavior with historical narratives. One of Putin's favorite narratives is that, throughout history, in spite of enemy attacks approaching from both sides of the country, Russia's strength has never waned.

> Putin's other favorite narrative is the historical justification for the centralized Russian state. In a 2012 article, Putin discussed the so-called national question. He argued that nationalism has come to the forefront in the West and that multiculturalism failed. He contrasts Western multiculturalism with Russia's imperial model, also a multicultural state, but hinging on the basis of the Russian people and Russian culture that are presented as somewhat superior to ethnic minorities living in Russia.[138]

This follows an article written by Putin on July 12, 2021, titled, "On the Historical Unity of Russians and Ukrainians." In the article Putin articulates how Ukrainians, Russians, and Belarusians are one people, which belong to the true Russia, with Russian and Ukrainians sharing a common culture and purpose.[139]

This is why an understanding of other countries' history and cultural identity gives us a better appreciation of who they are as we craft international and global policies. Far too often, US leaders forget this and believe everyone shares their viewpoint.

The famed historian Niall Ferguson stated that the US needs a Council of Historical Advisors to advise US presidents as they deal with world around us. Far too often, US presidents, whether Democrats or Republicans, often make decisions that have global consequences without fully understanding the region they are operating in.

> Speaking about his book, *Doomed to Succeed: The US–Israel Relationship From Truman to Obama*, the American diplomat Dennis Ross recently noted that "almost no administration's leading figures know the history of what we have done in the Middle East." Neither do they know the history of the region itself. In 2003, to take one example, when President George W. Bush chose to topple Saddam Hussein, he did not appear to fully appreciate either the

difference between Sunni and Shiite Muslims or the significance of the fact that Saddam's regime was led by a Sunni minority that had suppressed the Shiite majority. He failed to heed warnings that the predictable consequence of his actions would be a Shiite-dominated Baghdad beholden to the Shiite champion in the Middle East—Iran.

Political partisans will only examine the war in Iraq and US policy in the Middle East. The dangers of such limited views were brought to light in 2014, when President Obama was quoted in *The New Yorker* as saying, "I don't really even need George Kennan right now." Kennan was a historian and a diplomat during the Cold War. If Obama had studied George Kennan's philosophy, he would have had a better understanding of Ukraine's relationships with Russia and with Europe. Within two months after Obama's statement, "Russia had annexed Crimea."

> To address this deficit, it is not enough for a president to invite friendly historians to dinner, as Obama has been known to do. Nor is it enough to appoint a court historian, as John F. Kennedy did with Arthur M. Schlesinger Jr. We urge the next president to establish a White House Council of Historical Advisers. Historians made similar recommendations to Presidents Carter and Reagan during their administrations, but nothing ever came of these proposals. Operationally, the Council of Historical Advisers would mirror the Council of Economic Advisers, established after World War II. A chair and two additional members would be appointed by the president to full-time positions and respond to assignments from him or her. They would be supported by a small professional staff and would be part of the Executive Office of the President.[140]

On the other side of the globe, does the United States understand what shapes China and its leadership? Jeffrey A. Bader provided a detailed analysis of China's outlook in a paper, *How Xi Jinping Sees the World . . . and Why*. The following passages are from that study.

> Since the founding of the People's Republic of China in 1949, China has gone through a series of phases marked by sharply differing conceptions of what its leaders believe the international order should look like. These changing views reflect an underlying ambivalence toward the existing order, which has played out differently in different times. China is presently going through a new phase, whose meaning can be understood more fully if we

first understand how China's leaders got to where they are today in their thinking about the global order. Reflecting on both the continuity and the changes of these last seven decades will allow us to distinguish better what is genuinely new and different from what is familiar.

There is a temptation to see changes in a country's trajectory as reflecting the vision of the country's leader, in this case China's President Xi Jinping. Xi has already demonstrated that he is a decisive leader, stronger than his predecessor and determined not only to manage China but to transform it to meet huge unsolved challenges, primarily at home but also abroad. But in thinking about the potential impact of China's leader on a country of nearly 1.4 billion people, it is sometimes useful to recall that, in 1972 when President Nixon said to Chairman Mao that "the Chairman has changed the world," Mao famously replied, "No, I have just changed a few things on the outskirts of Beijing."

Mao's modesty on that occasion was excessive, and to be sure he and, to a lesser extent Xi have changed China's course. But his comment reminds us that large national transformations are more often the product of historical forces than the writ of one powerful leader. Understanding how Chinese views of international order since 1949 have evolved should help to clarify, not obscure, Xi Jinping's particular contributions to the way China sees and wishes to interact with the world.

Xi Jinping was an opportune figure to rethink China's approach to foreign policy presented by its new capacities. His father had been one of the giants of the Communist revolution and the first three decades of Communist rule, a comrade-in-arms of both Mao Zedong and Deng Xiaoping. Xi Jinping grew up enjoying the privileges of a Communist Party "princeling," and a consequent expedited road to success and power. But he, like his father, suffered the hardships imposed by the Cultural Revolution—exile from Beijing, lengthy interruption of his education, work in the countryside. When the Cultural Revolution ended, leading to the reform period ushered in by Deng Xiaoping, his career path included senior governing positions in China's more international-minded and economically progressive areas, notably Fujian and Zhejiang provinces and Shanghai. He emerged from the experiences of privilege and suffering with a firm faith in the necessity of a strong Communist Party to govern China, an aversion to chaos and social instability, a commitment to China's economic growth based on acceptance of the role of markets, and demand for respect for China internationally.[141]

In 2024, Hamid Lellou described Africa as "a key battleground in the global struggle between democracy and authoritarianism." His study, *US Relations with Africa and the New Cold War*, delves into the continent's complicated relationships with the rest of the world and sets the stage for how and why the various regions of Africa appeal to other powerful nations.

In recent decades, Africa has become a strategic focal point for major global powers, including China, France, Russia, and the United States, each vying for influence across the continent. These external players have impacted the political and security landscape in various African regions. In North Africa, instability following the Arab Spring drew attention from Western and Eastern powers. East Africa, with its strategic maritime routes and emerging markets, has seen increased engagement from China and the United States. West Africa, grappling with terrorism and economic challenges, has been a battleground for French and American counterterrorism efforts. The Sahel region faces severe security threats, exacerbated by military coups and the rise of jihadist groups. Central Africa's rich resources attract Chinese investment, while southern Africa, relatively more stable, remains a competitive ground for economic and political influence. Despite these engagements, many African countries struggle to achieve substantial benefits, often finding themselves entangled in the geopolitical maneuvers of these powerful nations.

China kept quiet and behaved as a silent pawn during the Cold War. During this time, it positioned itself globally and established deals that are proving its economic prowess and uncovering its long-term strategy. Today, China is the second-largest economic power, surpassing Japan and Europe and knocking at America's door. While the United States was fighting proxy wars in Africa, China was building an empire on the continent.

China's advantage in Africa is threefold:

- It does not defend universal human rights or try to leverage these principles when dealing with authoritarian regimes.

- It has an educated, skilled, low-cost workforce that is easily deployable for African infrastructure projects.

- It does not impose its cultural, political, or economic values on African nations.[142]

Does the United States understand Africa? According to most estimates there are almost two thousand different languages spoken in Africa, with Nigeria having about five hundred.

The US has to understand the strategic importance of the very complex and multi-dimensional African Continent. With fifty-four countries, four territories, and two independent states, the continent is the second largest in the world. Its young population (50 percent of the continent's 1.3 billion citizens are under age twenty-five) is rapidly growing in a technologically savvy environment.[143]

Africa is becoming an arena for great power competition, especially with China actively trying to exploit the vast resources the continent has to offer. Currently, the United States has a regional military command based in Stuttgart, Germany, as it tried to no avail to have the headquarters based on the African continent.

Each region of Africa is radically different from the others. Does the US understand the people and the distinct regions? Is the US listening, observing, and learning from the people of Africa? Are we speaking with tribal leaders, business leaders, and the citizens of each country? Do we have anyone that speaks each language and unique dialect? Have we partnered and brought on individuals from these countries to advise and provide subject matter expertise on policy issues? Do we understand the history of the African continent, including the pre-colonial, colonial, national liberation, and modern periods?

I was speaking with someone from South Africa, and he stated that America comes into the continent and pushes their vision of what Africa should be, where China doesn't care they just want the resources of the continent. How many share this view?

My conclusion is that a viable HUMIT intelligence operation would prove invaluable so we do not have a replication of the US being asked to leave a country, as was the case in Niger and Mali.

Seven

Cyber: The Battlefield of the Future

arfare is always evolving and changing. If you do not adjust to the changing dynamics, you will be left behind to your nation's detriment. Over a decade ago, former defense secretary, CIA director, White House budget director, and longtime member of Congress Leon Panetta warned of a "Cyber Pearl Harbor" that would cripple the US impacting businesses, critical key infrastructure, and even the military.

> The collected results of these attacks could be a cyber–Pearl Harbor — an attack that would cause physical destruction and the loss of life. In fact, it would paralyze and shock the nation and create a new, profound sense of vulnerability. A cyber-attack perpetrated by nation states or violent extremist groups could be as destructive as the terrorist attack of 9/11. Such a destructive cyber terrorist attack could paralyze the nation.[144]

Only a two short years ago, the FBI reported that Russian hackers have been scanning the systems of America's energy companies looking for vulnerabilities that could be exploited in any future conflict.

"The threat from Russia in a criminal sense, in the nation state sense, is very, very real - and current," said Bryan Vorndran, an assistant director in the FBI's cyber division, during a hearing before a US House of Representatives panel.[145]

Testifying before the Senate Armed Services Committee in April 2024, General Timothy D. Haugh stated:

> The United States and our allies face sophisticated cyber threats from both state and non-state actors. Malicious cyber actors are difficult to observe and attribute. The People's Republic of China (PRC) and the Russia Federation have integrated cyber-attack capabilities into military planning and operations to gain advantage during a crisis or conflict. In addition, Beijing, Moscow, and Tehran increasingly use social media and state-sponsored disinformation sites, both overt and covert, to shape narratives and sow confusion. We are particularly concerned with adversaries probing and exploiting our military and intelligence networks, compromising the US defense industrial base networks to steal weapon system technology and accessing or attempting to compromise US critical infrastructure. Additionally, our adversaries are targeting social media to coerce our personnel and monitor troop movements of US forces.

> The PRC is our pacing challenge. The PRC is the only competitor with the intent and, increasingly, the capacity, to reshape the international order. The PRC is our closest competitor in cyberspace and central to the global technology supply chain; it employs the world's largest cyberspace operations workforce and an even larger set of enablers in its defense, cybersecurity, and information technology industries. Russia's military and intelligence cyber forces are capable and persistent. Their focus on the conflict in Ukraine has diverted, but not ended, their worldwide intelligence and operational efforts in support of Moscow's foreign policy. Russian actors also attempt to divide Western allies and undermine them both abroad and internally. Moscow likely views the upcoming US election as an opportunity for malign influence and has previously targeted elections in the United States and Europe. We assess they will most likely do so again in this year's elections. Other nefarious actors such as Iran were brought up, to include North Korea.

> Strong partnerships with government, industry, academia, and foreign colleagues amplify our effectiveness and create advantages in turn for our partners. Our Components, when working in unison with diplomatic, military, law enforcement, homeland security, and intelligence capabilities, make a powerful combination that can disrupt the plans of malicious cyber actors wherever they hide. In addition, our Regional Cybersecurity and Engagement

Strategy in the Indo-Pacific will guide efforts with partners such as Australia, Japan, and South Korea to counter and contest foreign adversaries.[146]

I will address the critical need to have viable private-public partnership addressing cybersecurity later in this chapter. The following paragraphs highlight the vulnerabilities of cyber attacks on key infrastructure in the US.

In 2023, after years of persistently combating Russian cyber activities, the United States faced a variety of cyber-attacks Russia denied knowledge of groups such as the Callisto Group, Star Blizzard, and COLDRIVER, which all contributed to the attacks. However, everyone knows nothing happens in Russia without Russian complicity, especially when they are creating havoc toward the United States.[147]

In November 2024, Chinese hackers, dubbed Salt typhoon, breached eight major US telecommunications companies, to include telecom providers in almost two dozen countries, as part of Beijing's intelligence gathering operation. Many cyber security experts believe that this has been ongoing for the past two years, and the hackers were able to acquire call data and law enforcement surveillance request data, plus communications of individuals operating government and political activity.

China was also responsible for the 2015 data breach of The Office of Personnel Management (OPM), which was the largest data breach of government records in the history of the United States. The breach gained access to the personnel records of over 22 million Americans to include records of individuals working for the federal government, those specific individuals who had undergone background checks, to include their family and friends. The information obtained included personally identifiable information, that includes Social Security numbers, names, dates, and addresses of those trying to obtain a security clearance.

Former United states Attorney General Willaim P. Barr, delivering remarks on China Policy at the Gerald R. Ford Presidential Museum on July 16, 2020, stated, American firms face well-known obstacles in China's health market, including drug approval delays, unfair pricing limitations, IP theft, and counterfeiting. Chinese nationals working as employees at pharma companies have been caught stealing trade secrets both in America and in

China. And the CCP has long engaged in cyber-espionage and hacking of US academic medical centers and healthcare companies.

In fact, PRC-linked hackers have targeted American universities and firms in a bid to steal IP related to coronavirus treatments and vaccines, sometimes disrupting the work of our researchers. Having been caught covering up the coronavirus outbreak, Beijing is desperate for a public relations coup and may hope that it will be able to claim credit for any medical breakthroughs.[148]

Since Barr's remarks about the growing threat posed by China, The Chinese Communist Party has stolen between $400-600 billion in intellectual property each year. Much of what is stolen is used to further and enhance its military and surveillance expansion, which targets and threatens the United States.

A key aspect of this strategy is China's *Thousand Talents Program* (TTP), which is a program Beijing uses to "recruit overseas expertise to build up China's science and technology knowledge and innovation base." There have been several recorded instances of espionage activities instigated by the Chinese Communist Party.

In 2018, The Federal Bureau of Investigation (FBI) started the "Chinese initiative" to combat the Chinese Communist Party's ability to transfer information back to China. Through this initiative, various Chinese individuals working as US professors or employed at various companies sent key technology back to China.

China utilizes every aspect of its TTP program to gain access to key elements of the US economy. One other state-run program Beijing uses is the Overseas Chinese Scholars program, which sends 2. 1 million Chinese students across the globe. The very nature of this program is for Chinese nationals to study at foreign universities to gather knowledge and send it back home, and to enhance China's burgeoning science, technology, engineering, and math (STEM) fields.

These key technological transfers cost the US roughly $300 billion in lost revenue and the loss of millions of US jobs. Companies that do business in China are forced to relinquish their intellectual properties and partner with a Chinese company. The partnership includes teaching Chinese companies how to produce similar products and replicate the infrastructure.

What the US is now dealing with is major national security threats, especially from foreign state adversaries. In this case, America is facing China, who has been cyber-attacking the country. For decades, China has illegitimately been acquiring US academic research and information to advance their scientific, economic, and military development goals. China has an entire national strategy to steal intellectual properties, which saves Beijing "significant time, money, and resources while achieving generational advances in technology." Stolen research projects, plagiarism, elicitation, and overt thefts of intellectual and physical property give them a strategic advantage over the US and "deprive victimized parties of revenue and credit for their work."[149]

China's main focus is the theft of key technology, especially from the Department of Defense. In 2007, 2008, and 2011, investigators identified that Chinese hackers had penetrated the Pentagon servers, where a vast amount of data was illegally obtained. The data included blueprints of America's stealth fighters program and key supporting technology.

This major Achilles heel for the US is one which poses a major national security concern, and if left unchallenged, will erode the US's major advantage in military technology. China has developed a concentrated effort to cyber-attack, by hacking and gaining access to America's most sensitive military technology. Speculation is that China's newest advanced fighter aircraft is eerily similar to America's f-22 advanced fighter.

Richard Clark, a former US senior government official, believes that Chinese cyber espionage could result in the United States "having all of [its] research and development stolen"; Gen. Keith Alexander, a former director of the National Security Agency, worries that cyber espionage could lead to "the greatest transfer of wealth in history."[150]

To combat cyber attacks, the US Department of Defense developed a classified strategy detailed in the "2023 Department of Defense Cyber Strategy" which details how the Pentagon will protect the American people and advance defense priorities of the United States.

Since the strategy was launched in 2018, the Department of Defense has conducted various cyberspace operations to meet its objectives of disrupting malicious cyber attacks on the US key infrastructure. In 2022, The Russian military extensively used cyber capabilities in their invasion of Ukraine.

This armed conflict between the Russians and the Ukrainians demonstrated the importance of understanding the impact cyber capabilities have on the battlefield. In today's complex world, cyber-attacks are being employed by nation states and non-state actors, with cyber defense being employed by the private sector in thwarting their impact.

The United States must understand and continue to upgrade its cyber defense capabilities and pursue an offensive strategy against states and non-state actors' nefarious intention whether in a peace time mode or in actual armed conflict.

Far too often, the United States plays defense when our adversaries play offense regarding cyberwarfare. The US, especially the Department of Defense, has to understand that cyberwarfare will be the domain in which the US will be engaged in future combat. America needs not only to ready for conventional warfare, but for the next frontier in cyberspace. The Department of Defense cyber capabilities continue to evolve, but the US needs to rapidly improve, begin to play offense in cyber warfare, and stay ahead of our adversaries.

> As the Department's cyber capabilities evolve, so do those of our adversaries. Both the People's Republic of China (PRC) and Russia have embraced malicious cyber activity to counter US conventional military power and degrade the combat capability of the Joint Force. The PRC, in particular, sees superiority in cyberspace as core to its theories of victory and represents the Department's pacing challenge in cyberspace. Using cyber means, the PRC has engaged in prolonged campaigns of espionage, theft, and compromise against key defense networks and broader US critical infrastructure, especially the Defense Industrial Base (DIB). Globally, malicious cyber activity continues to grow in both volume and severity, impacting the US Homeland and placing Americans at risk.[151]

To address current and future cyber threats, the Department will pursue four complementary lines of effort:

Defend the Nation. The Department will campaign in and through cyberspace to generate insights about cyber threats. We will defend forward, disrupting and degrading malicious cyber actors' capabilities and supporting ecosystems. The Department will work with its interagency partners to leverage available authorities to enable the defense of US critical infrastructure and counter threats to military readiness.

Prepare to Fight and Win the Nation's Wars. The Department will campaign in and through cyberspace to advance Joint Force objectives. We will ensure the cybersecurity of the Department of Defense Information Network (DODIN) and conduct defensive cyberspace operations in order to protect it. The Department will enhance the cyber resilience of the Joint Force and ensure its ability to fight in and through contested and congested cyberspace. We will utilize the unique characteristics of cyberspace to meet the Joint Force's requirements and generate asymmetric advantages.

Protect the Cyber Domain with Allies and Partners. Our global Allies and partners represent a foundational strategic advantage for the United States. We will build the capacity and capability of US Allies and partners in cyberspace and expand avenues of potential cyber cooperation. We will continue to hunt forward operations and other bilateral technical collaboration, working with Allies and partners to illuminate malicious cyber activity on their networks. We will reinforce responsible state behavior by encouraging adherence to international law and internationally recognized cyberspace norms.

Build Enduring Advantages in Cyberspace. The Department will pursue institutional reforms to build advantages that will persist for decades to come. We will optimize the organizing, training, and equipping of the Cyberspace Operations Forces and Service-retained cyber forces. We will ensure the availability of timely and actionable intelligence in support of cyberspace operations and explore the intersection of emerging technologies and cyber capabilities. We will foster a culture of cybersecurity and cyber awareness, investing in the education, training, and knowledge development of personnel across the defense enterprise.

The Department of Defense views the People's Republic of China as one the greatest threats to United States They need to maintain and build on America's deterrence in the cyber world, as this is just one domain in which future warfighting will take place.

> The PRC seeks advantages in cyberspace to facilitate its emergence as a superpower with commensurate political, military, and economic influence. By exercising effective state control over businesses with large market share in the telecommunications, commercial hardware and software, and cybersecurity industries, the PRC tries to shape the global technology ecosystem. It exports dangerous cyber capabilities to like-minded nations and works to accelerate the rise of digital authoritarianism around the globe. Its efforts abroad are complemented by material strengths at home: a large technology industry and workforce, capable counterintelligence, and cybersecurity systems, and an array of proxy organizations empowered to pursue malicious cyber activity.

Beijing is currently utilizing cyber-attacks against the US and our allies. It routinely is engaged in pervasive intellectual property theft, conduct cyber intrusion and surveillance against the US and American citizens.

While China is definitely prepared for war, the US is vastly unprepared for the challenges ahead. Far too often, China's national security and military theories involve cyber warfare as a key component of the strategies against the US. This military doctrine of Beijing also targets America's key allies in the Indo-Pacific region.

> The PRC has undertaken significant military modernization and reorganization efforts in pursuit of this goal. In the event of conflict, the PRC likely intends to launch destructive cyber-attacks against the US Homeland to hinder military mobilization, sow chaos, and divert attention and resources. It will also likely seek to disrupt key networks which enable Joint Force power projection in combat.[152]

Beyond China, Russia has been cyber attacking the US for many years. Russia is doing everything it can by using cyber attacks to undermine the American people's confidence in its own elections.

The US cannot let its guard down, as other countries such as North Korea, Iran, and violent extremist organizations continue to threaten the United States. Each of these countries and criminal organizations has demonstrated and continue to push the envelope of varying levels of sophistication in their malicious cyber activity.

North Korea has always been a national security threat to the US. Previous use of conventional and nuclear forces has evolved into criminal objectives in cyberspace and espionage. Malicious cyber activity through the use of ransomware and compromised cryptocurrency wallets is the new criminal objective. North Korea's cyber targets include media outlets, colleges and universities, and government entities throughout the world.

> Iran's aggression and sponsorship of illicit activities extends into cyberspace. Iran has used malicious cyber activity to conduct espionage, interfere in political processes, and punish actors that Iran deems hostile to its interests. During the 2020 US election cycle, Iran demonstrated the use of novel tactics, techniques, and procedures (TTPs) in its malign influence efforts against the United States. Iran's malicious cyber activity against the US , Israel, and other nations indicates an increased willingness to target countries with comparatively stronger warfighting capabilities.

> Violent extremist organizations have seen their capabilities largely degraded by more than two decades of counterterrorism operations conducted by the United States and our Allies and partners. While these actors effectively used social media for the purposes of recruitment, propaganda, and command and control, they have not yet demonstrated the ability to conduct significant or sustained malicious cyber activity against the United States.[153]

Beyond nation state actors, transnational criminal organizations are also utilizing cyberspace by threatening the financial well being of companies and individuals with attacks to include ransomware and other malicious attacks. The company I currently work for was hit with a ransomware cyber-attack in the fall of 2024. This attack crippled the company for a month, forcing the company to lose millions of dollars in lost revenue and severely crippled productivity.

In 2020, Cybercrime Magazine report that "If it were measured as a country, then cybercrime—which is predicted to inflict damages totaling $6 trillion USD globally in 2021—would be the world's third-largest economy after the US and China." The same article continued:

> Cybersecurity Ventures expects global cybercrime costs to grow by 15 percent

per year over the next five years, reaching $10.5 trillion USD annually by 2025, up from $3 trillion USD in 2015. This represents the greatest transfer of economic wealth in history, risks the incentives for innovation and investment, is exponentially larger than the damage inflicted from natural disasters in a year, and will be more profitable than the global trade of all major illegal drugs combined.[154]

On a national scale, cybercrime costs the US economy hundreds of billions of dollars annually. In 2023, the estimated cost was around $320 billion (Astra Security). In 2024, the cost is projected to be significant, with cybercrime damage costs continuing to rise globally, emphasizing the growing threat of cyberattacks.

Cyberattacks come in various forms, each with unique methods and impacts. Here are some of the most common types:

1. Phishing

Phishing attacks involve cybercriminals impersonating legitimate organizations to steal sensitive information. These attacks account for nearly 39. 6% of all email threats and can lead to identity theft, financial fraud, and unauthorized access to secured systems (Express VPN).

AI-Driven Phishing: Cybercriminals are leveraging publicly available and custom-made AI tools to orchestrate highly targeted phishing campaigns. These AI-driven phishing attacks craft convincing messages tailored to specific recipients, using proper grammar and spelling to increase the likelihood of successful deception and data theft.

2. Ransomware

Ransomware encrypts a victim's files, rendering them inaccessible until a ransom is paid. The average cost of a ransomware attack is around $4. 54 million, including recovery costs averaging $1. 85 million. These attacks often target entire networks, leading to significant financial and operational disruptions.

3. Distributed Denial of Service (DDoS)

DDoS attacks overwhelm online services with traffic from multiple sources, causing service disruptions. In 2023,

DDoS attacks increased significantly, particularly targeting retail, shipment, and public relations websites.

4. Data Extortion

In data extortion attacks, cybercriminals steal sensitive data and threaten to release it unless a ransom is paid. This type of attack poses a significant threat to both individuals and businesses, as it involves theft and potential public exposure of sensitive information.

Voice and Video Cloning: In addition to traditional phishing tactics, malicious actors increasingly employ AI-powered voice and video cloning techniques to impersonate trusted individuals, such as family members, co-workers, or business partners. By manipulating and creating audio and visual content with unprecedented realism, these adversaries seek to deceive unsuspecting victims into divulging sensitive information or authorizing fraudulent transactions.[155]

A technological revolution is reshaping the US economy. Fourth Industrial Revolution (4IR) technologies have emerged with "the potential to make our infrastructure more sustainable, efficient, and connected while enabling once-futuristic ideas such as 'Smart Cities' and autonomous transportations." However, these seemingly perfect improvements could threaten our national security. A hacker could potentially infiltrate a country and control not only the digital assets, but the physical infrastructure as well. The increases in cybersecurity are matched by new developments in cyberattacks. Although some experts recommend instituting public-private partnerships as a means of identifying and confronting deficiencies in our cybersecurity, others remain concerned that such relationships could lead to even more division and cybercrimes.[156]

If the United States is to be successful at preventing and disrupting cyber attacks on America from either nation state actors, non-states, and transnational criminal organizations, it will need to have a holistic public-private approach. The United States have some of the best digital technological companies in the world and there is no reason the US should not utilize the immense talent of these companies to combat cyber-attacks. It's to the mutual benefit of both the private and public sector to combine the immense resources and talent of both sectors.

Considering 85 percent of the nation's critical infrastructure is owned by the private sector, with the nation's leading corporations producing most of the software and hardware used by the Department of Defense and government agencies. The innovation and performance by the private sector make it essential for it to be involved in how the United States combats cyber-attacks against the US.

Testifying before The Senate Armed Forces Committee, General Timothy D. Haugh stated:

> Enhancing the security of government, private sector, and critical infrastructure systems grows ever more imperative. Foreign adversaries continuously update how they operate, and frequently work through American-owned networks and devices. USCYBERCOM works in partnership with the Military Department's Counterintelligence organizations, the FBI-led National Counterintelligence Task Force, and DHS's Cybersecurity and Infrastructure Security Agency (CISA), sharing actionable intelligence that helps counter adversary activities, making them more expensive and less consequential. Consistent with Congressional support, USCYBERCOM is sharing information with industry to help bolster their ability to defend themselves against exploitation by malicious cyber actors, and to share more broadly the insights that both our industry partners and we gain from our collaboration. Our UNDERADVISEMENT program, a voluntary collaboration with dozens of private partners, links cybersecurity expertise across industry and government. It has led to dozens of operational successes to impose costs on our adversaries, and enabled network owners to eradicate the threats from their systems. Due to the foresight of Congress, USCYBERCOM has enhanced authority to share information with private sector information technology and cybersecurity entities, enabling industry to defend itself better.[157]

One issue for the US government is that, in 2019, Microsoft employees wrote a letter to their leadership demanding the company stop working on all products for the US military.

The employees stated, "we did not sign up nor did we agree to develop technology to be used by the US to further increase the armed forces lethality." The workers emphasized that they wanted to have input into the intended uses and purposes of the software they were creating.[158]

The letter was intended as a critique of Microsoft building and designing weapons of war, and it was not stated if these same employees would be against collaboration with the Department of Defense or other federal agencies as it relates to cyber security. Not known is how these same employees feel about Microsoft's significant presence inside China, and its many collaborations with the Chinese Communist Party, especially utilizing its software for surveillance and military apparatus.

Microsoft is a multinational, billion-dollar corporation and a technological company, with its operating software found in over 72 percent of all desktop operating systems. Microsoft has also faced difficulties in dealing and working with China. This would seem to be a logical fit for America's largest software company to part of a private-public partnership in preventing cyber-attacks against the US. Microsoft would also be part of revolutionizing the US educational system by partnering with the US government in establishing technical trade schools in the K-12 system and further enhancing follow on training after a student graduates high school could further their education in technological training programs to obtain relevant certifications that would include cyber security training.

Google is another company that has had its employees refuse to work with the Department of Defense. A contract regarding the $1.2 billion Project Nimbus was slated to be used by the Israeli government and military. Amazon had partnered with Google on this. Many Google employees objected because they felt it was going to be used against Palestinians.

> Google, hoping to head off a rebellion by employees upset that the technology they were working on could be used for lethal purposes, will not renew a contract with the Pentagon for artificial intelligence work when a current deal expires next year. Diane Greene, who is the head of the Google Cloud business that won a contract with the Pentagon's Project Maven, said during a weekly meeting with employees on Friday that the company was backing away from its AI work with the military, according to a person familiar with the discussion but not permitted to speak publicly about it. Google's work

with the Defense Department on the Maven program, which uses artificial intelligence to interpret video images and could be used to improve the targeting of drone strikes, roiled the internet giant's work force. Many of the company's top AI researchers worried that the contract was the first step toward using the nascent technology in advanced weapons.[159]

General Timothy D. Haugh in his posture statement regarding future plans for DOD cyber security, stated:

All of these efforts begin with people. We must hire and retain the right talent and keep our personnel ready to meet the challenges of competition and conflict in and through cyberspace and the information environment. We are working to grow uniformed cyber leaders at all levels, up to and including the officers who will eventually succeed me in this post. The staffing and training of our teams improves every year, and the Command's cyber readiness system is now able to ingest data directly from the Defense Readiness and Reporting System without manual input. USCYBERCOM's authorities as Joint Cyberspace Trainer will enable Joint training standards across the entire Department, boosting its ability to defend networks while enabling CMF teams to focus on hunting and contesting foreign adversaries. Additionally, over the past year, we have worked to fill our civilian billets, driving down security and personnel processing times by 25 percent and accelerating hiring actions to fill more than 250 vacancies across the Command. We are using special hiring authorities offered in 10 US C. 4092 to attract top technical talent to join USCYBERCOM. We have made job offers to key experts and look forward to hiring more in 2024. Indeed, we are maximizing use of DoD Cyber Excepted Service authority to streamline civilian hiring and offer competitive employment incentives.[160]

The United States needs a better public-private partnership to deal with cyber-attacks against the country. Almost all the largest technology companies in the world are located in the United States, so seeking advice and partnership with companies like Apple, Nvidia, Microsoft, Google, and others makes sense. As I mentioned in Chapter three, this is an opportunity to expand educational opportunities for Americans in this country.

Generation Z was the first generation born during the technological revolution. They were the first to grow up using solely digital technology for communication, conducting business, and even in their personal lives. Now a new generation of young people, the Alpha generation, are right behind them. We are failing the country by failing to embrace the massive technological skills which have been ingrained in these two generations.

As I mentioned in Chapter Three, it is a common belief that in order for all students in K-12 to be successful they must attend a college or university. When they graduate, they are faced with massive amounts of student loan debt and worthless degrees that do not provide for a viable economic future. Washington needs to partner with the private sector and revamp America's failing public school system by embracing and embedding a viable technological educational curriculum into the K-12 system.

America's K-12 public educational system should have a three-prong focus. The first is to prepare students who want the traditional educational focus of going to a college or university. A second focus would be to train students in the building/manufacturing trades. These key skills are needed for hundreds of thousands of jobs right now. The third focus would be to establish technological training programs in the K-12 system. Upon graduation, these students would then attend technological training schools to gain various certifications and then be placed into the private and public sector economy.

Speaking with an owner of a major cyber security company, I asked him if a college degree was necessary for a career in the cyber security field. His answer was a resounding no! You just need the temperament to work in that type of career field. The same was asked of the owner of a drone company. He repeated the same as the previous owner. No college degree is needed, only the disposition to be able to work in this field. By forcing a major revamping of America's beleaguered and dysfunctional public educational system with a viable, robust technological, we would be strengthening the nation's national security. Failure to do so would lead us to a "cyber Pearl Harbor," and if this happens, our security is forever compromised.

Eight

Energy Security is National Security

Energy has become a top national security concern for the United States, and all through the 2024 US presidential election both Democrats and Republicans had far different views on how to obtain energy security.

The International Energy Agency (IEA) defined energy security as "the uninterrupted availability of energy sources at an affordable price." Most economists and business leaders would articulate it as being able to consistently power the US economy for a reasonable price without fear of disruption or elimination of that energy source or sources. In 2024, policies by Washington and various state governments were trying to do away with one source of reliable energy to replace it with one that has dubious ability to produce the energy needed to power the US economy now and into the future.

Energy independence is now different from the past. It traditionally was focused on oil supply, in which oil prices were determined by global market forces. Other factors go into oil prices, such as global events, geopolitical conflicts, unanticipated increases in electricity demand, extreme weather conditions, and the global demand of booming global economies affect prices. Additional factors go into energy security, such as minerals, manufacturing dependence, and cyber security.

Based on the amount of oil, natural gas, and electricity from solar and wind, America is the most likely country in the world to claim energy independence. Although China is the world's largest producer of wind and solar energy, the US is the second-largest, and produces more oil and natural gas than any other nation. However, what is lacking to have true energy security is "the availability of reliable and reasonably priced energy." US energy security is improving as supply chains become steadier, disruptions are minimized, and sources of energy are made more readily available across the country.

America's technological revolution in the energy sector placed the US on the trajectory in becoming energy independent.

After years of painstaking trial and error, entrepreneurs developed and perfected the technology to extract oil and gas from shale rock. Until the late 1990s and early 2000s, experts did not believe this was possible. Once computer-assisted horizontal drilling was developed, more rock could be accessed than the previous vertical oil wells. Once pressurized water, sand, and chemicals are injected into the horizontal pipe, the dense rock is broken down. Through this process, known as *fracking*, oil and gas enter the well and rise to the surface. Modern fracking also uses 3-D seismic imaging to explore under the surface.

This advance in technology and American innovation has made the United States the world's largest producer of natural gas, almost double the second-largest natural gas producer, Russia.

Russian President Vladimir Putin was concerned that America's revolutionary shale energy production would be a game-changer and cede the energy sector advantage to the United States. He was outraged that fracking gave the US a stronghold on energy and reduced Russia's control of the gas industry. Industry professionals attending a 2013 international economic conference in St. Petersburg recall that when shale gas was brought up, Putin "erupted in fury, denouncing shale as barbaric, dangerous, and environmentally destructive." It was evident that he viewed the extraction of oil and gas through fracking in the United States, as "a direct threat to Russia's power."[161]

Democrats and the Biden administration pursued policies into eliminating fossil fuels in favor of renewable energy by placing the United States on the unsustainable path towards electrifying the country. This was all pushed forward despite the mountains of evidence that renewable energy could never provide the energy needed to power the US economy forward, and would only cede America's energy security to China. Republicans, and now President Trump, have a far different approach by focusing on the natural energy that is so abundant in this country, which means utilizing all forms of energy, including fossil fuel.

"Energy security is national security, as one does not exist without the other."[162] No matter how much we want to withdraw from fossil fuel, it will be the staple for the American economy for the foreseeable future. For the US economy to grow, it will still have to rely on fossil fuel. Failure to address this reality will only consign the US to outsourcing its national security to others, namely China.

The cost of transitioning to a "Green New Deal," as advocated by the Democratic Party, will have enormous costs for the United States. This cost has never been fully debated. In 2019, Rep. Alexandria Ocasio-Cortez (D-NY) and Sen. Ed Markey (D-Mass.) introduced legislation detailing a "Green New Deal" that aims to reduce carbon emissions and fundamentally remake the US economy.

Since the progressive elements of the Democratic Party first officially announced "The Green New Deal" in 2018, the entire Democratic Party has been focused on eliminating fossil fuels and replacing it with renewable energy. The Aspen Institute report at the American Action Forum (AAF) provided its expertise on how this would impact the American economy.

The Green New Deal (GND) is a sweeping policy plan, setting out ambitious objectives for energy and economic policy. In keeping with the American Action Forum's (AAF) mission to analyze, evaluate, and educate on issues of important public policy, a group of its experts, myself included, published a report exploring the potential cost of six elements of the GND: (1) a Low-Carbon Electricity Grid, (2) a Net Zero Emissions Transportation System, (3) Guaranteed Jobs, (4) Universal Health Care, (5) Guaranteed Green Housing, and (6) Food Security. We provided a range of estimates for each element. If one adds up the low end of the range, the total is $52 trillion (over the next 10 years); at the high end it is $93 trillion.[163]

Throughout President Biden's time in office, his administration had an ongoing war against domestic hydrocarbon production. This placed America's energy security, and its national security, in real jeopardy. US elected officials and other entities who are zealously pursuing this new green utopia have to factor in the ramifications of their decision and its impact on the US economy. Far too often, history is rife with examples of how the pursuit of an idea, even with the best intentions, can cause the greatest disaster. It is imperative that leaders comprehend the consequences of ignoring "the fundamental physical realities that create the context in which policies are implemented."

America is entering uncharted territory. This singular pursuit of renewable energy is not practical in powering the energy needed for a modern economy such as the United States.

An energy transition away from gas and oil would cause America to become energy dependent on other countries. Germany agreed to shut down its nuclear reactors. This decision led to an increase in energy consumption and forced the country to rely on its adversary, Russia, to supply the needed energy. Once its reactors were shut down in 2022, Germany's insistence on pushing its new green policies through denuclearization created even more of a need for Russian gas, coal, and oil. This should be a lesson to America on what happens when a country fails to explore the implications of ill-conceived but well-intended energy decisions.

It was only a few short years ago when President Doanld Trump scolded European leaders. Germany, which failed to invest 2 percent for its own defense, relied on the United States for their protection from potential Russian aggression, but then signed lucrative energy deals with Moscow for their energy needs. With Russia's invasion of Ukraine, Germany depends heavily on Russian natural gas to fuel its economy.

This dependency on Russian energy undermined the West's response and further hampered deterrence to Russia's expansionist push over the past decade. With Russia's invasion of Ukraine, Moscow has punished Germany and the rest of Europe by substantially cutting off natural gas deliveries The end result is that Europe is now facing a full-blown energy crisis with high natural gas prices. This has substantially increased inflation and thrown the European economy into a recessionary period. In 2023, the Institute for Energy Research(IER) reported:

> While Germany and others are seeking out alternative hydrocarbon sources, they will be unable to fully make up the shortfall from lost Russian supplies in the near or medium term. Natural gas is a particularly vexing problem, as it can only be transported via one or two ways: pipelines in its original gaseous form or by being liquified and transported overseas as liquified natural gas (LNG). The process of turning natural gas into LNG and utilizing it for electricity production requires substantial infrastructure, of which Germany has almost none. At the same time, alternative oil suppliers (like Canada, the United States, or Saudi Arabia) are operating at close to capacity and simply cannot produce and transport enough to provide for all of Europe's energy demand.

Although it is apparent that President Trump will not be eliminating all fossil fuels, the US should be wary of falling into the same trap as Germany. The IER report continued:

> Due in large part to government intervention, the United States is becoming progressively more reliant on electric vehicles (EVs) and nonnuclear renewable energy sources for its transportation and energy needs. These technologies rely on a large input of rare earth metals and other mined elements, particularly lithium and cobalt, the supply of which is dominated almost entirely by the People's Republic of China (PRC). These same minerals are also key inputs in the production of many advanced weapons systems, like fighter jets and ballistic missile defenses, that are critical for a robust national defense.[164]

Before the United States takes the great leap forward and fully embraces the "New Green Deal" and the electrification of the country, one again just needs to examine the German experiment. Only a few short years ago, Germany had a dynamic economy and was the leading economic power in Europe, but that all has faded from memory for most Germans.

Right now, Germany is lagging and on the verge of a severe recession, the worst not seen since the end of the Second World

War. The three factors that have placed Germany in this precarious situation have everything to do with energy. The first being disruption of natural gas imports from Russia, since Moscow's invasion of Ukraine, the closing of existing nuclear power plants, and the transition to renewable energies.

Germany's thriving, vibrant manufacturing sector used to be the envy of Europe. Now, it is only an empty shell of its former self. The country is finding it difficult to produce enough energy to provide electricity for the remaining businesses, and its citizens face the highest utility cost in Europe. Economically, Germany had started to recover after COVID–19, but was cut off from its main energy supplier when Russia's war with Ukraine began. A resistance to nuclear energy and inability to quickly transfer to green energy compounded Germany's economic crisis.[165]

Germany was all in on transitioning to renewables, but bureaucratic delays, permitting problems, and other issues had the country move too fast, as renewables could never supply the energy needed to power a modern manufacturing-based country.

Another example is right here in the United States. California Governor Gavin Newsom is doing everything he can to eliminate fossil fuel and replace it with renewable energy such as wind and solar. The problem is that many items that Americans use and consume every day are made from derivatives of crude oil.

Besides all the obvious things derived from crude oil — gasoline, diesel fuel, av gas, kerosene, propane, butane, and all plastics used in hospitals and food storage — our homes are full of products derived from petroleum in their production. Things like construction materials such as roofing and housing insulation, linoleum flooring, furniture, appliances, and home decor such as pillows, curtains, rugs, and house paint. Even much of our clothing and our shoes use petrochemicals in their manufacture. Oh, and how about basketballs, golf balls, and bags, football helmets, surfboards, skis, tennis rackets, and fishing rods? And where would we be without soap, shampoo, and toothpaste?[166]

Governor Gavin Newsom is hell-bent on taxing the energy sector out of existence in favor of renewable energy. Not only will this fail to produce the desired results, but consumers and the business community will feel the impact and pay the ultimate price. Californians pay the highest price for utilities in the country, and this has made the citizens poorer as a result.

The governor must be made to understand that fossil fuels can not only be used for electricity generation, but to make thousands of products we use in our daily lives. Without the forethought of what replaces crude oil in manufacturing, we will only inflict massive shortages and substantially increase inflation because of the scarcity of these products. Merchant ships and jets are also dependent on fuels manufactured from crude oil. Right now California imports more crude oil from overseas than any other state in the US, and much of it emanates from the Middle East.

> By continually decreasing in-state oil production, Newsom's energy policies continue to force California, the fifth largest economy in the world, to be the only state in contiguous America that imports most of its crude oil energy from foreign countries. That dependence, via maritime transportation from foreign nations for the state's crude oil energy demands, has increased imported crude oil from 5 percent in 1992 to almost 60 percent today of total consumption.[167]

California is now dependent on other nations. These countries are not always friendly to the United States, thus creating major national security threat. Additionally, well-paying manufacturing jobs and business opportunities in California are reduced.

The California governor has been doing everything he can to move the golden state away from fossil fuels in favor of renewable energy, in the form of solar and wind. In keeping with his new green push in 2020, Newsom signed an executive order that cemented moving the state away from fossil fuels. The governor claimed that renewable energy would create jobs and contribute to the growth of the economy. So far, evidence has shown the opposite is happening. Additionally, in keeping with this green obsession the governor signed an executive order requiring all new passenger vehicles to be zero-emission by 2035, and with it, he added the elimination of harmful emissions in transportation.[168]

In December 2024, The US Environmental Protection Agency approved California's landmark environmental plan to ban and end the sale of gasoline-only powered vehicles by 2035.

As the state races to eliminate gas-powered vehicles in favor of electric vehicles, the problem they will face but have never addressed is the cost, especially for low-income families. The other issue is the lack of convenient and functioning charging stations, and the distance that zero-emission vehicles can travel between charges, especially in rural areas of the state.

Secretary of Transportation Pete Buttigieg was asked in 2024, why only eight charging stations had been built since the 2021 Infrastructure and Jobs Act was passed. The total allocated for charging stations was $7.5 billion, with $5 billion through the National electric Vehicle Infrastructure Formula Program or NEVI, and $2.5 billion distributed through the Charging and Fueling Infrastructure Discretionary Grant Program, or CFI. This was to create 500,000 charging stations by 2030. Why did they have so few after a few years, and how did they plan to reach the number the Biden administration wanted?

Even with California's zero-emission mandate that no gas-powered vehicles could be purchased, there still would be millions of gas- and diesel-fueled vehicles on the road. They pushed for closure of the refineries. How would the state maintain available fuel for those vehicles as it indirectly forced refineries to reduce their output?

How can California generate enough electricity to recharge millions of zero-emission vehicles from wind and solar alone, when both are intermittent energy sources? They can capture the bulk of energy when the sun shines and the winds blow. Unfortunately, the usage of energy peaks in the evening, the opposite of when energy is captured from wind and solar.

With the movement toward Artificial Intelligence (AI), all of the data centers will need an enormous amount of electricity to maintain a climate control environment. Where does all this energy come from if you eliminate fossil fuels and solely rely on renewable energy? This was another question California never addressed.

Despite being unable to produce enough electricity for the state, California is leading the effort to push a very aggressive "green agenda," such as banning the sale of gas-powered vehicles. During the summer of 2022, California's Air Resource Board required all new vehicles sold in California to be free of greenhouse gases by 2035. Then, days later, the California Independent System Operator issued a warning not to power your electric vehicle because it would place a strain on the electrical grid during the heat wave the state was experiencing.

If the state can't produce enough electricity now, how will it handle the increased demand in the future? A report in 2024 outlined several of the causes of increased energy demand.

> Data centers could account for 44% of US electricity load growth from 2023 to 2028, followed by about 27% from the residential sector, 17% from manufacturing and the remainder from the commercial sector.

> By 2028, US utilities may need to increase annual energy generation by between 7% and 26% above 2023 levels in order to meet projected demand, the consulting firm said. "That's far beyond the largest five-year generation boost of about 5% that US utilities achieved from 2005 through 2023,"

> Concern is growing regarding AI and its demand for electricity. Data centers could consume 9% of the United States' electricity generation by 2030—double the amount consumed today, the Electric Power Research Institute said in May. US data center load is expected to grow to nearly 21 GW this year, up from 19 GW in 2023, according to a Federal Energy Regulatory Commission report.

As California and the Democratic Party push the nation to embrace the electrification of America, the question is, where do we get all the rare earth minerals needed for battery production when we do not produce that in the US?

China is doing everything it can to corner the market on rare earth minerals. Therefore, in December of 2024, Beijing put forth strict limits on exports of technologies that could be used for both civilian and military applications. The communist nation is doing everything it can to ban shipments of antimony, gallium, and germanium, and for the first time in history, specifically restricted these minerals from exportation to the United States, without restricting them to other countries. This action directly linked mineral security with the ensuing trade war.

These restrictions come on the heels of the release of an updated Dual-Use Export Control List by China's Ministry of Commerce. The list expands and consolidates a list of items deemed to have dual civilian and military uses. This update framework introduces a unified system and facilitates stricter oversight to tighten China's export controls. This list not only streamlined the implementation of this export controls but leaves the door open for China to implement new export bans on other strategic minerals on the list such as tungsten.[169]

These restrictions have a great impact on US national security, as gallium, germanium, and antimony are key components for defense technologies. The Chinese are making significant investments in these areas, especially in munitions, and obtaining top of the line weapons systems and equipment that far exceed those of the United States.

Antimony is one of the key elements needed for US national security. Since 1990, when the last US antimony mine was closed, America has imported all of its antimony from other countries. The silvery-white metal is found in the earth's crust, and is a type of ore that, when mixed with other metals, is used militarily in everything from bullets to night-vision goggles. It is also used in lead-acid batteries. China is the largest producer of Antimony, and other essential elements, such as cobalt and uranium.

Today, China has an effective monopoly on all of the rare earth elements and in particular, two heavy rare earths: dysprosium and terbium. It has also taken a mercantilist approach to a slew of strategic elements in the Periodic Table, including nickel, cobalt, copper, lithium, and tellurium. In addition, it has a near-monopoly on the production of neodymium-iron-boron (NdFeB) magnets, which are used in electric vehicles, wind turbines, and numerous consumer and military applications . . . China is "putting the screws to us."[170]

With all this in mind, a 2023 report noted that throughout Biden's presidency, he worked "to impose an Energiewende-style transition on the United States by subsidizing the market share of renewable energy sources and increasing the regulatory burden on conventional sources." At the time, 12 percent of America's energy came from a growing renewable energy supply.

However, renewables need far higher mineral inputs than their hydrocarbon counterparts. An electric vehicle (EV), for example, requires six times the mineral resources than does a similar gasoline-powered car. While some of this demand can be filled by familiar metals like nickel, copper, and aluminum, less common minerals like lithium and cobalt play a key role, as do many so-called "rare earth" elements. According to the International Energy Agency (IEA), the decarbonization process will cause the demand for these critical minerals to explode.[171]

All we are doing is exporting America's energy security to China and placing US national security in jeopardy.

As mentioned earlier in this chapter, this is the national security dilemma for the United States: The Chinese Communist Party (CCP) dominates the global supply chain for all of the key minerals and other strategic metals which go into any renewable applications for electrification of the US economy.

The key threat to America's national security is that the US is far more dependent on Chinese imports for its renewable energy sources of key rare earth minerals than it ever was on the Middle East for its oil supplies.

According to the US Geological Survey, the United States is 100 percent import dependent for at least 20 critical and strategic minerals (not including the "rare earths"), and between 50 percent and 99 percent dependent for another 30 key minerals. For example, the United States is totally dependent on imports for vital strategic metals that are necessary components for military weapons systems, cellphones, solar panels, lithium-ion batteries, and many high-technology products. The reason for this dependency is not due to geologic impediments, but due to politics. Large portions of public lands in the West have not been sufficiently explored, and permitting in the United States takes seven to ten years compared to two or three years in Australia and Canada.

As the United States charts a course on eliminating fossil fuels as an energy source in favor of renewable energy, it must understand that some of the best intentions, no matter how meaningful, have had disastrous consequences. If the United States continues in its relentless push to develop renewable energy sources to power electric vehicles at the expense of traditional energy sources, it will only be acquiescing US energy security to China, who currently dominates the infrastructure needed for the electric energy market to sustain itself.

> The first Trump administration issued a policy directive, "A Federal Strategy to Ensure Secure and Reliable Supplies of Critical Minerals," which directs the development of a strategy to reduce reliance on foreign sources for critical minerals, such as rare-earth elements, and promoting policies to increase US critical mineral development. The goal is to open up federal lands and streamline the permitting process so that the United States can mine these resources. The US Mining Association estimates that the United States is endowed with over $6 trillion in these resources, which could add $50 billion to the economy every year.

> This executive order instructed Secretary Zinke, in coordination with then Secretary of Defense James Mattis, to identify and publish a list of critical minerals, and develop a strategy to reduce the United States' import reliance for these increasingly important ingredients to modern personal and military devices.[172]

In addition to a list, President Trump instructed them to develop a plan for the future, including reducing dependence on critical minerals, an analysis of the processes for recycling technologies, and improving access for mineral exploration in the US. Secretary Zinke commented:

> The fact that previous administrations allowed the United States to become reliant on foreign nations, including our competitors and adversaries, for minerals that are so strategically important to our security and economy is deeply troubling. As both a former military commander and geologist, I know the very real national security risk of relying on foreign nations for what the military needs to keep our soldiers and our homeland safe.[173]

Throughout Biden's time as president, he had been waging a perpetual war with America's domestic energy producers. Hopefully, this will end with the Trump presidency, but it will take work to repair the damage. The Biden administration targeted the energy industry with "burdensome regulations and rhetorical assaults" that not only contributed to the energy crisis but drove the US to become dependent on foreign energy. "The shale revolution made the United States energy independent, but the federal government must get out of the business of picking winners and losers in energy, must stop retarding investment in oil and natural gas, and must allow market forces to drive production."[174]

> When it comes to replacing reliable, weather-independent, 24/7 coal or gas plants, the intermittency of solar and wind farms simply doesn't fill the need. Some early adapters of intermittent renewable energy like California and Germany are seeing the problem already. It comes in the form of grid instability and blackouts. As a result, California is cutting back new solar way back, keeping gas plants running, and postponing the planned shutdown of the Diablo Canyon nuclear plant. California businesses and wealthy homeowners are buying diesel generators.

> Solar and wind, when properly integrated can, and will, make a significant contribution to carbon reduction. But the backbone of any robust system must be reliable 24/7 (Baseload) power. And the problem is much bigger than just replacing existing fossil plants. America's reindustrialization, along with the electrification of transportation, heating, and industry, will double or triple electrical demand before 2050. It will take massive new energy generation to meet that challenge. Our nation still needs to come up with a plan to meet that projected increase in baseload with 24/7 energy.[175]

There is another question to consider. How will the average American afford electric vehicles? Prices in 2024 were outrageous.

> The average price for a brand-new EV is over $60,000, about $12,000 more than the average four-door sedan. Even with tax credits, it is hard to see how consumers come out ahead, at least for now. The electric version of the base version of the Ford F-150 pickup truck, the best-selling vehicle in America, costs an additional $26,000 over the gasoline-powered variety. EVs are not affordable for most Americans: it's little wonder that only 16 per cent of them are seriously considering a purchase.

With the current push for electric vehicles by environmental advocates have to be asked the question, is America prepared for the consequences to the nation's automobile sector and the residual companies that support it? China will very soon overtake the Western auto industry. China already outpaces the United States in the production of Electric vehicles.[176]

If current trends in automobile sales continue, and as American consumers abandon electric vehicles, and environmental groups push their elected officials in states and in Washington on this path, are they prepared for the devastation to the US auto industry and the elimination of millions of union jobs in states like Michigan?

> Nearly 900,000 workers are responsible for manufacturing large auto parts or systems and assembling final internal combustion engine vehicles at original equipment manufacturers (OEMs) and Tier 1 suppliers, according to data analyzed from the US Bureau of Labor Statistics (BLS). These vehicles are powered by burning gasoline as opposed to EVs, which rely on electric motors and battery packs instead of internal combustion engines and components like fueling and exhaust systems. As components within powertrain systems are expected to be the source of the greatest manufacturing differences between the two types of vehicles, it's expected that there will be significant implications for these workers.
>
> Supply chain jobs that are linked to parts only relevant to internal combustion engine vehicles such as engines and fuel injection systems, may have the greatest risk of displacement as more EVs are produced. Of the more than 886,000 workers at OEMs and Tier 1 suppliers — firms that manufacture large parts or systems and assemble final vehicles — close to 58,000 workers focused on gasoline engines and engine parts manufacturing are likely to experience the most severe employment impacts. Fifty-seven percent of those workers are located in Michigan, Ohio, Indiana, Tennessee and Kentucky.[177]

The push to electrify the country will have devastating impacts on the very communities in which Democrats claim to want to help. In California, Governor Newsom's push to eliminate gas-powered vehicles will have extreme unintended consequences. How will low-income and middle-income individuals afford electric vehicles? They can barely afford gas powered vehicles now because of inflation.

The electric vehicle fixation could soon undermine the state's last great blue-collar sector, the heavily unionized ports of Los Angeles, Long Beach, and Oakland. International trade, including exports and imports, supports nearly 5 million California jobs, nearly one in four of the state totals. If California proceeds to ban gas trucks and forces port transport to turn to electric trucks, this will make transportation far more expensive. Electric trucks can go at best 80 miles without stopping, whereas a less expensive, low-emission gas truck can cover 500, greatly increasing efficiency.

Those advocating the push to the electrification of the nation's economy have never addressed how this impacts the manufacturing, logistics, and agriculture sectors of the American economy, which employs millions of workers, often at good wages. What happens to their job prospects?

Epilogue

The global landscape has dramatically changed since the end of the Cold War. The U.S. is no longer a hegemonic power without any near peer competitor. Currently, the United States will have to function in a multi-power international environment which is reminiscent of the great power competition of the 19th century. The United States still is the world's most dominant political, economic and military power, but other countries such as China are trying to challenge the U.S. and if it's plausible replace the U.S. as the world's global superpower.

After twenty years of continuous wars in the Middle East region, China watched as the US was preoccupied with the war on terror and commenced a massive military build up. Beijing's promise was to bring its renegade province of Taiwan back into the fold under a one China authority. The other aim of China is by 2049, the 100th anniversary of the Chinese Communist Party (CCP), is to be the world's dominant superpower where all political, military and economic power runs through Beijing.

Currently, America's adversaries view the United States as a diminished superpower heading in the direction of past global empires, which declined and were replaced by a more powerful country, in this case China. Our adversaries have witnessed America spend massive amounts of treasure and human capital in the Wars throughout the Middle East, notably in Iraq, Afghanistan, and Syria. For all the focus on the Middle East, and with the vast expenditure in treasure and the lives of its sons and daughters, the US has little to show for it. As the ongoing conflicts in the region, the US was forced to maintain a viable naval and troop presence in Syria, Iraq and the surrounding area.

Over the past few years, our adversaries and allies witnessed in real time America's humiliating withdrawal from Afghanistan, the continued conflict in Ukraine, coupled with ongoing wars in the Middle East which America seems powerless to stop. Every statement by former President Joe Biden while he served as president was rejected by our allies and adversaries alike. This further rebuke led many to conclude America is a declining superpower.

With the return of the Trump presidency, many view a return to American deterrence. President Trump campaigned on his America first approach and has clashed with the US more traditional allies, especially with European countries who are part of the NATO alliance. This was never more apparent over US policy toward Ukraine. President has often clashed with NATO countries over military spending and underfunding Ukrainian support in its fight against Russia.

America now faces a multipolar world, with countries vying to supplant the U.S. as the world's dominant superpower; in this case, China. China, despite its rapidly expanding military, faces massive internal problems themselves. China has to deal with a rapidly shrinking population, massive truculent debt, and disproportionately high corruption that goes all the way up to the highest level of the Chinese Communist Party leadership. Despite all this, America faces its own internal issues.

For too long America has rested on its laurels and allowed areas to decline, which in this case is its economy and the US massive national debt crisis. The US needs to revitalize its economy and a major national security threat is America's inability to end its prolific spending, and get its fiscal house in order. Both Republican and Democrats have pushed programs that were never fully paid for or had dubious and unrealistic funding mechanisms that proved faulty over time. In each case America's national debt skyrocketed to astronomical heights, which now is over $36 trillion and growing substantially. The current political climate in Washington is extremely toxic, especially now that Trump is back in the White House. Neither party is budging from any perceived compromise over how to reduce the federal budget and begin to reduce the massive government federal debt.

President Trump added more controversy with his Department of Government Efficiency (DOGE), led by billionaire entrepreneur Elon Musk. This agency was tasked with ridding the federal government of waste fraud and abuse of taxpayer money. It began with an auspicious start, but it has uncovered billions in wasteful government spending. To many Washington insiders the cure may be worse than the disease, but to average Americans, they are all rooting out corruption of tax dollars in Washington.

Both political parties have failed to even mention how they would reduce America's national debt! The biggest time bomb for America is its unsustainable entitlement programs of Social Security, Medicare, and Medicaid, which will be insolvent in less than ten years if current trends continue. Right now at the beginning of the Trump presidency, as both Republicans and Democrats debate the future of the federal budget, neither side has even remotely presented policy on how they would tackle let alone reform the nation's entitlement programs of Social Security, Medicare, and Medicaid. All we get is repeated attacks by both Democrats and Republicans against how the other side is destroying these popular programs.

All during the 2024 presidential election, former president Donald Trump consistently spoke for the need for tariffs to be placed not only against China with its massive trade surplus with the US, but our allies as well. Now that Trump is back as president he has placed tariffs on China and allies such as Canada, Europe, and Mexico, as these nations have placed undue burdens on American manufacturing. Trump has stated he believes in free trade, but it must be fair trade! Democrats have been highly critical of Trump's tariff policy, as they believe it will ignite a trade war and place undue burden on the American consumer with higher prices.

The other concern for America is trying to revitalize its manufacturing sector, but one of the key problems is that many states pursue toxic anti-business policies. Currently, the largest states in the US, California, New York, and Illinois are making it extremely difficult for businesses to thrive, let alone operate. California has been at the forefront of anti-business policies, and current trends in its progressive ideology are continuing to make the golden state a business desert. One piece of legislation moving its way through the California state legislature, is to mandate oil companies to pay for the cost of fire related damage from wildfires. The belief by California elected officials is that fossil fuels contribute to shifts in the climate, which then results in catastrophic fires that have impacted the state. If this takes hold in California, it will only make Californians pay a much higher price for utilities than they already do and will send businesses fleeing in droves to other low-cost energy states.

The current situation in Illinois, New York, and other progressive run states makes owning, operating, and starting a business extremely difficult. Far too often, they push a progressive business ideology in the guise of helping the working class, but in reality, it only creates a lack of employment opportunities, and only contributes to a vast income inequality.

One of the US most glaring weaknesses in the revitalization of American manufacturing is America's failing education system. Far too much money from the federal, state, and local level is allocated to K-12 education and the only results we have is that half of American children cannot read nor do math to grade level and it's even worse for ethnic minorities in the country. The current debate is centered around the elimination of the US Department of Education and transferring its responsibilities back to the states as in the past. Many red states are challenging the status quo by enacting school choice, voucher programs, charter schools and having parents having a greater voice in how their child is taught, what curriculum is taught, and by whom.

The biggest challenge for America is the extreme dysfunction in the country, but especially in Washington, with both political parties treating politics as a zero-sum game with the goal to win at all costs, and by any means necessary. The moniker has become the ends justify the means! With Trump now back in as president, Democrats are doing everything they can to resist the Trump administration. The opposition to Trump is coming from all sides as the opposition to his administration are utilizing every tool they can to include weaponizing the US judicial system in lawfare and having a partisan media violate journalistic ethics all in the name of their perception of saving Democracy.

This current lawfare against the Trump administration has now elevated the opposition by attacking the legitimacy of the US Supreme Court. Much of this stems from the high court overturning Roe vs Wade, and returning the debate back to the states for citizens to decide at what point a woman is allowed to have an abortion. In Trump's first term, he appointed three justices to the US Supreme Court. In the opposition's mind, this changed the balance decidedly into a solid majority conservative court. In the past few years the US Supreme Court has issued controversial rulings on the environment, immigration, and federal government regulatory enforcement, and in each case it ruled that the legislative branch makes the law, the executive branch enforces the law and the US Supreme Court interprets the constitutionality of the laws and enforcement. The opposition is aghast at these decisions, and they have openly stated we need to add more justices to the court, to alter the makeup and place age or term limits on the justices.

As the Trump presidency begins, its governing an element has taken hold for decades but has really upended what makes Democracies different from authoritative countries and that is an independent media. The current environment has the media now providing advocacy journalistic reporting instead of just providing the facts. Just examine the difference in media coverage of President Trump compared to President Joe Biden. If the media is truly the watchdog against government maleficence, why hasn't the media looked deeper into the wasteful spending practices of many government agencies, to include USAID spending practices? Why hasn't the media asked why any of the inspector generals investigated any of these egregious spending, with many of the spending going back to Democratic leaders and their families?

As the Trump administration begins to reshape US foreign policy, the president is beginning to adjust and fundamentally alter how American foreign policy is conducted and does it meet US national security objectives. One of the first policy directives the Trump administration embarked on was to unleash DOGE into examining how US taxpayers' money is currently being spent, one such target being the United States Agency for International Development (USAID). The president's efficiency department highlighted many millions of dollars of egregious spending on various dubious areas that many Americans find extremely questionable.

Currently, US foreign policy under the new Trump presidency is in the process of fundamentally recalibrating everything to align it with America's strategic strategy. One of the first places the Trump administration started with was the United States Agency for International Development (USAID). With DOGE and Elon Musk looking at every aspect of federal spending, what was found shocked many Americans. The agency was spending on extreme progressive projects across the globe, to include transgender surgeries in Guatemala, and $1.5 million to promote LGBTQ job opportunities in Serbia.

This re-altering of U.S. foreign policy extends to the Department of Defense, where President Trump campaigned on by eliminating DEI (Diversity, Equity, and Inclusion) programs throughout the US military. Once in office, he had his Secretary of Defense Pete Hegseth issue Department of Defense end any and all DEI programs. This push to end DEI training extended to the president relieving the Chairman of the Joint Chiefs of Staff, The Chief of Naval Operations and other senior level military commanders who have embraced President Biden's DEI initiatives while he served as president.

US intelligence is another area where the Trump administration is focusing on by tapping former Democratic presidential candidate and Democratic congressional representative Tulsi Gabbard to recalibrate how the 18 intelligence agencies collect and analyze intelligence information in an unbiased manner. This change to US intelligence will be a work in progress and we will have to examine the results as crises unfold across the globe.

The Trump administration is coming back to the presidency and will be entering a world far different from the one he left the presidency in 2021. The current global conflict is precarious as the US now has to deal with a multipolar world with China, Russia, and Iran challenging the rules-based order established by the United States after the Second World War. President Trump is having to deal with conflicts in Ukraine, the ongoing war in Gaza, and for that matter across the Middle East.

This is coming at a time where American deterrence is not what it used to be, and the world now looks at the US as a diminished power, not the hegemonic behemoth it was a few decades ago. Currently, the US military spends too much on non-essential programs and is not focused on the various contingencies should they arise. How the US handles the multipolar world and how it can establish its global power will ensure peace and tranquility not only for the US but for the world. If the US cannot reestablish its global power and only diminishes over the decades, then the US and the world will face a far different future.

Works Cited

Allison, Graham, and Niall Ferguson. 2016. "Why the President Needs a Council of Historians." *Harvard Kennedy School Belfer Center for Science and International Affairs*. September. https://www.belfercenter.org/publication/why-president-needs-council-historians.

Anesta, Kaylee. 2024. "Spending Per Pupil in Public Schools Averaged $15,633, Up 8.9% in FY 2022." *United States Census Bureau*. April 25. https://www.census.gov/library/stories/2024/04/public-school-spending.html.

Bader, Jeffrey A. 2016. "How Xi Jinping Sees the World…and Why." *Brookings Institute*. July. https://www.brookings.edu/wp-content/uploads/2016/07/xi_jinping_worldview_bader-1.pdf.

Baltimore City Public Schools. 2024. "Dr. Sonja Santelises agrees to extend contract as City Schools CEO to June 2026." *Baltimore City Public Schools*. October 22. https://www.baltimorecityschools.org/article/1835410.

Baron, Ethan. 2018. "H-1B: Foreign citizens make up nearly three-quarters of Silicon Valley tech workforce, report says." *The Mercury News*. May 8. https://www.mercurynews.com/2018/01/17/h-1b-foreign-citizens-make-up-nearly-three-quarters-of-silicon-valley-tech-workforce-report-says/.

Barr, William P. 2020. "Attorney General William P. Barr Delivers Remarks on China Policy at the Gerald R. Ford Presidential Museum." *Archives U.S. Department of State*. July 16. https://www.justice.gov/archives/opa/speech/attorney-general-william-p-barr-delivers-remarks-china-policy-gerald-r-ford-presidential.

Baskaran, Gracelin, and Meredith Schwartz. 2024. "China Imposes Its Most Stringent Critical Minerals Export Restrictions Yet Amidst Escalating U.S.-China Tech War." *Center for Strategic & International Studies*. December 4. https://www.csis.org/analysis/china-imposes-its-most-stringent-critical-minerals-export-restrictions-yet-amidst.

Bergmann, Max, Michael Kimmage, Jeffrey Mankoff, and Maria Snegovava. 2024. "America's New Twilight Struggle with Russia."

Foreign Affairs. March 6. https://www.foreignaffairs.com/russian-federation/americas-new-twilight-struggle-russia?check_logged_in=1.

Blank, Marion. 2023. "Two Thirds of American Kids Can't Read Fluently." *Scientific American*. September 26. https://www.scientificamerican.com/article/two-thirds-of-american-kids-cant-read-fluently/.

Borshchevskaya, Anna. 2021. *Putin's War in Syria: Russian Foreign Policy and the Price of America's Absence*. I.B. Tauris.

Brown, Michael. 2023. "Department of Defense Budgeting: The Unrecognized National Security Threat." *Defense Budgeting for a Safer World: The Experts Speak*. Comps. Michael J. Boskin, John Rader and Kiran Sridhar. Hoover Institution Press, November 1. http://efaidnbmnnnibpcajpcglclefindmkaj/https://www.hoover.org/sites/default/files/research/docs/17-Boskin_DefenseBudgeting_ch10.pdf.

Bruhl, Joe. 2022. "America Ignores Africa at Its Own Peril." *War on the Rocks*. June 14. https://warontherocks.com/2022/06/america-ignores-africa-at-its-own-peril/.

Bryce, Robert. 2024. "China Runs the Table." *Robert Bryce*. December 7. https://robertbryce.substack.com/p/china-runs-the-table?utm_campaign=email-post&r=3prtm&utm_source=substack&utm_medium=email.

Brzezinski, Zbigniew. 1997. *The Grand Chessboard*. Perseus Book Group.

Budinger, Bill. 2024. "Why Renewables Cannot Replace Fossil Fuels." *Democracy A Journal of Ideas*. February 16. https://democracyjournal.org/arguments/why-renewables-cannot-replace-fossil-fuels/.

Bushnell, Lauren. 2021. "Educational Disparities Among Racial and Ethnic Minority Youth in the United States." *Ballard Brief*. Spring. https://ballardbrief.byu.edu/issue-briefs/educational-disparities-among-racial-and-ethnic-minority-youth-in-the-united-states.

Camera, Lauren. 2019. "U.S. Students Show No Improvement in Math, Reading, Science on International Exam." *U.S. News & World Report*. December 3. https://www.usnews.com/news/education-news/articles/2019-12-03/us-students-show-no-improvement-in-math-reading-science-on-international-exam#google_vignette.

Cancian, Mark F., Matthew Cancian, and Eric Heginbotham. 2023. "The First Battle of the Next War: Wargaming a Chinese Invasion of Taiwan." *Center for Strategic & International Studies*. January 9. https://www.csis.org/analysis/first-battle-next-war-wargaming-chinese-invasion-taiwan.

Center for an Informed Public University of Washington. 2023. *What we can learn from Finland*. March 1. https://www.cip.uw.edu/2023/03/01/finland-media-literacy/.

Center on Budget and Policy Priorities. 2023. *Policy Basics: Non-Defense Discretionary Programs*. November 14. https://www.cbpp.org/research/federal-budget/non-defense-discretionary-programs.

Chambers II, John Whiteclay. n.d. ""Wild Bill" Donovan and the Origins of the OSS." *National Park Service*. https://www.nps.gov/articles/wild-bill-donovan-and-the-origins-of-the-oss.htm.

Chivvis, Christopher S., Jennifer Kavanagh, Sahil Lauji, Adele Malle, Sam Orloff, Stephen Wertheim, and Reid Wilcox. 2024. "Strategic Change in U.S. Foreign Policy." *Carnegie Endowment for International Peace*. July 23.

Chodkowski, William M. 2012. "What was USIA?: Overview, Mission, Structure." *The United States Information Agency*. November. https://www.americansecurityproject.org/ASP%20Reports/Ref%200097%20-%20The%20United%20States%20Information%20Agency.pdf.

Churchill, Winston. 1996. *My Early Life: 1874–1904*. Scribner.

Ciphertex Data Security. 2024. *The Cost of Cyber Theft to the U.S. Economy in 2024: Projected to Exceed $350 Billion*. May 24. https://ciphertex.com/2024/05/24/the-cost-of-cyber-theft-to-the-u-s-economy-in-2024/.

Clark, Bryan. 2020. "Pentagon And Congress Risk Bungling Drive To Modernize U.S. Military." *Forbes*. July 8. https://www.forbes.com/sites/bryanclark/2020/07/08/pentagon-and-congress-risk-bungling-drive-to-modernize-us-military/.

Clausewitz, Carl Von. 1976. *On War*. Princeton: Princeton University Press.

Cordesman, Anthony H. 2020. "Ending America's Grand Strategic Failures." *Center for Strategic and International Studies*. June 22. https://www.csis.org/analysis/ending-americas-grand-strategic-failures.

—. 2022. "The New Biden National Security." *Center for Strategic and International Studies*. October 14. https://www.csis.org/analysis/new-biden-national-security.

—. 2017. "U.S. Military Spending: The Cost of Wars." *Center for Strategic and International Studies*. July 10. https://www.csis.org/analysis/us-military-spending-cost-wars.

Dabrowski, Ted, and John Klinger. 2022. "Poor student achievement and near-zero accountability: An indictment of Illinois' public education system – Wirepoints Special Report." *Wirepoints*. June 1. https://wirepoints.org/poor-student-achievement-and-near-zero-accountability-an-indictment-of-illinois-public-education-system-wirepoints-special-report/.

Daniels, Seamus P. 2024. "What a Continuing Resolution Could Mean for Defense Funding in FY 2025." *Center for Strategic and International Studies*. September 24. https://www.csis.org/analysis/what-continuing-resolution-could-mean-defense-funding-fy-2025.

Davis, Daniel L. 2013. "Purge the generals." *Armed Forces Journal*. August 1. http://armedforcesjournal.com/purge-the-generals/.

DeBatto, David. 2020. "The Death (and possible rebirth) of HUMINT in America." *Lansing Institute*. June 24. https://lansinginstitute.org/2020/06/24/the-death-and-possible-rebirth-of-humint-in-america/.

Devermont, Judd. 2024. "Human Geography Is Mission-Critical." *War on the Rocks*. October 15. https://warontherocks.com/2024/10/human-geography-is-mission-critical/.

Dickson, Paul. 2020. "Marshall's Secret Preparations for War." *American Heritage*. September. https://www.americanheritage.com/marshalls-secret-preparations-war.

Dunlop, Richard. 2014. *Donovan: America's Master Spy.* Skyhorse.

Ernst, Douglas. 2019. "Jeh Johnson says border crisis is real: 'I cannot begin to imagine' 4K apprehensions per day." *The Washington Times*. March 29. https://www.washingtontimes.com/news/2019/mar/29/jeh-johnson-says-border-crisis-is-real-i-cannot-be/.

Federal Bureau of Investigation. 2019. "China: The Risk to Academia." *FBI*. https://www.fbi.gov/file-repository/counterintelligence/china-risk-to-academia-2019.pdf/view.

First Liberty Institute. 2024. "Radical Court "Reform" Will Destroy a Judicial System That's Worked for 230+ Years." *First Liberty*. August 23. https://firstliberty.org/news/court-reform-will-destroy-the-judicial-system/.

Flickinger, Glenn. 2017. "The Man Who Made Ike." *Veterans Breakfast Club*. https://veteransbreakfastclub.org/the-man-who-made-ike/.

Funaiole, Matthew P., Brian Hart, Joseph S. Bermudez Jr., and Samantha Lu. 2023. "Tracking China's Naval Modernization at Key Shipyards." *China Power*. November 21. https://chinapower.csis.org/analysis/china-naval-modernization-jiangnan-hudong-zhonghua-shipyard/.

Garrity, Patrick J. 2021. "Military Education and Mentorship: Fox Conner and Dwight Eisenhower." *Classics of Strategy and Diplomacy*. March 26. https://classicsofstrategy.com/2021/03/26/military-education-and-mentorship-fox-conner-and-dwight-eisenhower/.

Gates, Robert M. 2010. "Letter from Secretary of Defense Dr. Robert M. Gates to Chairman of the Senate Budget Committee Kent Conrad." *U.S. Department of State Diplomacy in Action.* April 21. https://2009-2017.state.gov/secretary/20092013clinton/rm/2010/04/140674.htm.

Gates, Robert. 2010. "Text of Speech by Robert Gates on the Future of NATO." *Atlantic Journal.* June 10. https://www.atlanticcouncil.org/blogs/natosource/text-of-speech-by-robert-gates-on-the-future-of-nato/.

Ghaffary, Shirin. 2019. "Microsoft workers are demanding the company cancel its $480 million contract with the US military." *Vox.* February 22. https://www.vox.com/2019/2/22/18236290/microsoft-military-contract-augmented-reality-ar-vr.

Gilli, Andrea, and Mauro Gilli. 2018/19. "Why China Has Not Caught Up Yet: Military-Technological Superiority and the Limits of Imitation, Reverse Engineering, and Cyber Espionage." *MIT Press Direct.* Winter. https://direct.mit.edu/isec/article/43/3/141/12218/Why-China-Has-Not-Caught-Up-Yet-Military.

Grablick, Colleen. 2022. "Math Proficiency Rates Plummeted, Achievement Gap Widened In D.C. Schools During Pandemic." *DCist.* September 2. https://dcist.com/story/22/09/02/dc-standardized-test-results-achievement-gap/.

Grabow, Colin. 2019. "Rust Buckets: How the Jones Act Undermines U.S. Shipbuilding and National Security." *Cato Institute.* November 12. https://www.cato.org/policy-analysis/rust-buckets-how-jones-act-undermines-us-shipbuilding-national-security.

Gunness, Kristen, and Phillip C. Saunders. 2022. "Averting Escalation and Avoiding War: Lessons from the 1995–1996 Taiwan Strait Crisis." *National Defense University.* December. https://digitalcommons.ndu.edu/china-strategic-perspectives/2/.

Haddick, Robert, Elaine Luria, and Mark Montgomery. 2024. "Quarantines and Blockades." *The Boiling Moat.* Edited by Matt Pottinger. Hoover Institution Press, July 1. http://

efaidnbmnnnibpcajpcglclefindmkaj/https://www.hoover.org/
sites/default/files/research/docs/11_BoilingMoat_Ch8.pdf.

Hamilton, Alexander. 1788. "Federalist No. 78 The Judiciary
Department." *Library of Congress*. https://guides.loc.gov/
federalist-papers/text-71-80.

Hamre, John J., Joyce Bongongo, Kate Macfail, John Schaus, and
Nina Tarr. 2024. "A Strategic Framework for America in the Twenty-
First Century: The Brzezinski-Zinke Project." *Center for Strategic
and International Studies*. September.

Hanson, Victor Davis. 2025. "Conspiracies Too Awful to
Imagine?" *American Greatness*. January 6. https://amgreatness.
com/2025/01/06/conspiracies-too-awful-to-imagine/.

Haugh, Timothy D. 2024. "Posture Statement of General Timothy
D. Haugh 2024." *U.S. Cyber Command*. April 12. https://www.
cybercom.mil/Media/News/Article/3739700/posture-statement-
of-general-timothy-d-haugh-2024/.

Hernandez, Jennifer. 2021. "Green Jim Crow, How California's
Climate Policies Undermine Civil Rights and Racial Equity." *The
Breakthrough Institute*. August 16. https://thebreakthrough.org/
journal/no-14-summer-2021/green-jim-crow.

Hill, Bryce. 2024. "Illinois Forward 2024: A Sustainable State
Budget Plan." *Illinois Policy*. November 23. https://www.
illinoispolicy.org/reports/illinois-forward-2024-a-sustainable-
state-budget-plan/.

Holtz-Eakin, Doug. 2019. "How Much Will the Green New Deal
Cost?" *Aspen Institute*. June 11. https://www.aspeninstitute.org/
blog-posts/how-much-will-the-green-new-deal-cost/.

Hughes, Dana. 2013. "George W. Bush's Legacy on Africa Wins
Praise, Even From Foes." *ABC News*. April 26. https://abcnews.
go.com/blogs/politics/2013/04/george-w-bushs-legacy-on-africa-
wins-praise-even-from-foes.

IN Homeland Security Staff. 2012. "American Public University
Edge." *American Public University Edge*. October 22. https://
apuedge.com/facing-a-cyber-9-11-could-it-really-happen/.

Institute for Energy Research. 2018. "The United States Is Dependent on Other Nations for Critical and Strategic Minerals." *Institute for Energy Research.* February 23. https://www. instituteforenergyresearch.org/international-issues/united-states-dependent-nations-critical-strategic-minerals/.

Jones, Seth G. 2024. "China Is Ready for War." *Foreign Affairs.* October 2. https://www.foreignaffairs.com/china/china-ready-war-america-is-not-seth-jones?check_logged_in=1.

Kang, Choi, and Peter K. Lee. 2024. "Why U.S. Naval Power Needs Asian Allies." *War on the Rocks.* January 12. https:// warontherocks.com/2024/01/why-u-s-naval-power-needs-asian-allies/.

Kennan Institute. 2024. "Remembering George F. Kennan." *Wilson Center.* March 1. https://www.wilsoncenter.org/article/ remembering-george-f-kennan.

Khan, Farhan. 2024. "The Decline of U.S. Global Power and the Rise of a Multipolar World." *India Today.* October 3. https://www. indiatoday.in/global/story/the-decline-of-us-global-power-and-the-rise-of-a-multipolar-world-2610676-2024-10-03.

Khvostunova, Olga. 2024. "Putin's Warped Idea of Russian History." *Foreign Policy Research Institute.* February 27. https:// www.fpri.org/article/2024/02/putins-warped-idea-of-russian-history/.

Kilcullen, David, interview by Vincent Bernard. 2011. *Interview with David Kilcullen* (June 7). http:// efaidnbmnnnibpcajpcglclefindmkaj/https://international-review. icrc.org/sites/default/files/irrc-883-interview.pdf.

Kirby, John F., and Kenneth F. McKenzie Jr. 2021. "General Kenneth F. McKenzie Jr. Commander of U.S. Central Command and Pentagon Press Secretary John F. Kirby Hold a Press Briefing." *U.S. Department of Defense.* September 17. https://www.defense.gov/ News/Transcripts/Transcript/Article/2780738/general-kenneth-f-mckenzie-jr-commander-of-us-central-command-and-pentagon-pres/.

Kotkin, Joel. 2024. "America's Working Class is Back in Control." *Spiked Online*. December 1. https://www.spiked-online. com/2024/12/01/americas-working-class-is-taking-back-control/#google_vignette.

—. 2024. "Electric cars will decide the outcome of the American election." *The Telegraph*. March 26. https://www.telegraph.co.uk/ us/comment/2024/03/26/china-electric-vehicles-joe-biden-ira-green-energy/.

—. 2024. "Elon Musk and Woke Capital are in a Battle for the Future of America." *Joel Kotkin*. October 18. https://joelkotkin. com/elon-musk-and-woke-capital-are-in-a-battle-for-the-future-of-america/.

—. 2024. "Joel Kotkin: Western Nations Cripple their Economies with Green Initiatives While China and Others Laugh." *National Post*. October 15. https://nationalpost.com/opinion/joel-kotkin-western-nations-cripple-their-economies-with-green-initiatives-while-china-and-others-laugh.

—. 2024. "Why both sides are right in the H-1B visas row." *Spiked Online*. December 30. https://www.spiked-online. com/2024/12/30/why-both-sides-are-right-in-the-h-1b-visas-row/.

Lasley, Shane. 2018. "Critical minerals order." *Mining News*. January 1. https://www.miningnewsnorth.com/story/2018/01/01/ news/critical-minerals-order/109.html?m=true.

Ledford, Joseph. 2024. "America Must Put The "Americas First"." *Hoover Institution*. December 9. https://www.hoover.org/ research/america-must-put-americas-first.

Lehr, Jay, and Tom Harris. 2023. "The End of oil Would be the End of Civilization." *America Out Loud News*. January 9. https:// www.americaoutloud.news/the-end-of-oil-would-be-the-end-of-civilization/.

Lellou, Hamid. 2024. "US Relations with Africa and the New Cold War." *US Army War College Publications*. November 21. https:// publications.armywarcollege.edu/News/Display/Article/3974676/ us-relations-with-africa-and-the-new-cold-war/.

Lontay, Oliver. 2024. "Germany's Energy Crisis: Europe's Leading Economy is Falling Behind." *Harvard International Review.* May 30. https://hir.harvard.edu/germanys-energy-crisis-europes-leading-economy-is-falling-behind/.

Lynch, Sarah N. 2022. "FBI Says Russian Hackers Scanning U.S. Energy Systems and Pose 'Current' Threat." *Carrier Management.* March 31. https://www.carriermanagement.com/news/2022/03/31/234435.htm.

Marr, Jack, John Cushing, Brandon Garner, and Richard Thompson. 2008. "Human Terrain Mapping: A Critical First Step to Winning the COIN Fight." *Military Review.* March–April. https://www.armyupress.army.mil/Portals/7/PDF-UA-docs/Marr-2008-UA.pdf.

McKay, Tom. 2024. "Intel to Lay off 15% of Workforce after Ugly Quarterly Report." *IT Brew.* August 7. https://www.itbrew.com/stories/2024/08/07/intel-to-lay-off-15-of-workforce-after-ugly-quarterly-report.

Miller, Matthew. 2023. "U.S. Takes Action to Further Disrupt Russian Cyber Activities." *US Department of State.* December 7. https://2021-2025.state.gov/u-s-takes-action-to-further-disrupt-russian-cyber-activities/.

Morgan, Steve. 2020. *Cybercrime To Cost The World $10.5 Trillion Annually By 2025.* November 13. https://cybersecurityventures.com/cybercrime-damages-6-trillion-by-2021/.

Moussa, Emad. 2022. "The Mista'arvim: Israel's notorious undercover agents." *The New Arab.* April 18. https://www.newarab.com/analysis/mistaarvim-israels-notorious-undercover-agents.

Mullen, Michael. 2011. *Posture Statement of Admiral Michael G. Mullen, USN Chairman of the Joint Chiefs of Staff Before the 112th Congress Senate Appropriations Subcommittee on Defense.*

Musk, Elon, and Vivek Ramaswamy. 2024. "Elon Musk and Vivek Ramaswamy: The DOGE Plan to Reform Government." *The Wall Street Journal.* November 20. https://www.wsj.com/opinion/musk-and-ramaswamy-the-doge-plan-to-reform-government-supreme-court-guidance-end-executive-power-grab-fa51c020?st=DueQ9H.

National Security Archive Electronic Briefing Book No. 207. 2006. "Post-Saddam Iraq:." *The National Security Archive*. November 4. https://nsarchive2.gwu.edu/NSAEBB/NSAEBB207/index.htm.

Newsom, Gavin. 2020. "Governor Newsom Announces California Will Phase Out Gasoline-Powered Cars & Drastically Reduce Demand for Fossil Fuel in California's Fight Against Climate Change." *Governor Gavin Newsom*. September 23. https://www.gov.ca.gov/2020/09/23/governor-newsom-announces-california-will-phase-out-gasoline-powered-cars-drastically-reduce-demand-for-fossil-fuel-in-californias-fight-against-climate-change/.

Noonan, John. 2024. "Trump Prepares a Pentagon Plucking Committee." *National Review*. November 12. https://www.nationalreview.com/corner/trump-prepares-a-pentagon-plucking-committee/.

Ochmanek, David A., Anna M. Dowd, Stephen J. Flanagan, Andrew R. Hoehn, Jeffrey W. Hornung, Michael J. Lostumbo, and Michael J. Mazarr. 2023. "How to Reverse the Erosion of U.S. and Allied Military Power and Influence." *Rand*. July 25. https://www.rand.org/pubs/research_reports/RRA2555-1.html.

Office of Budget Policy and Analysis. 2023. *Nation's Report Card Underscores New York's Need for Academic Recovery.* March. https://www.osc.ny.gov/reports/nations-report-card-underscores-new-yorks-need-academic-recovery.

Office of the New York State Comptrollers. 2024. *DiNapoli Releases Report on SFY 2024–25 Financial Plan.* July 19. https://www.osc.ny.gov/press/releases/2024/07/dinapoli-releases-report-sfy-2024-25-financial-plan.

Okail, Nancy, and Matthew Duss. 2024. "America Is Cursed by a Foreign Policy of Nostalgia." *Foreign Affairs*. December 3. https://www.foreignaffairs.com/united-states/america-cursed-foreign-policy-nostalgia?check_logged_in=1.

O'Rourke, Roland. 2024. "Great Power Competition: Implications for." *Congressional Research Service*. August 28. https://www.congress.gov/crs-product/R43838.

Papst, Chris. 2024. "23 Baltimore schools have zero students proficient in math, per state test results." *Fox 5 News*. January 31. https://foxbaltimore.com/news/project-baltimore/state-test-results-23-baltimore-schools-have-zero-students-proficient-in-math-jovani-patterson-maryland-comprehensive-assessment-program-maryland-governor-wes-moore.

Patrick, Stewart. 2024. "BRICS Expansion, the G20, and the Future of World Order." *Carnegie Endowment for International Peace*. October 9. https://carnegieendowment.org/research/2024/10/brics-summit-emerging-middle-powers-g7-g20?lang=en.

Peck, Gabriel. 2024. "California's Fiscal Outlook." *The California Legislature's Non-Partisan Fiscal and Policy Advisor*. November 20. https://www.lao.ca.gov/Publications/Report/4939.

Peter G. Perterson Foundation. 2024. "How is K–12 Education Funded." *Peter G. Peterson Foundation*. August 19. https://www.pgpf.org/article/how-is-k-12-education-funded/.

Peter G. Peterson Foundation. 2024. *Continuing Resolutions Are Stopgap Measures — But Now We Average Five a Year*. November 9. https://www.pgpf.org/article/continuing-resolutions-were-designed-to-be-stopgap-measures-but-now-we-average-five-a-year/.

Project 2025. 2023. "Mandate for Leadership The Conservative Promise." *Project 2025 Presidential Transition Project*. Edited by Paul Dans and Steven Groves. Washington, DC: The Heritage Foundation. http://efaidnbmnnnibpcajpcglclefindmkaj/https://static.project2025.org/2025_MandateForLeadership_FULL.pdf.

Putin, Vladimir. n.d. "Article by Vladimir Putin "On the Historical Unity of Russians and Ukrainians"." *Presidential Library*. https://www.prlib.ru/en/article-vladimir-putin-historical-unity-russians-and-ukrainians.

Ray, Charles A. 2021. "Does Africa Matter to the United States?" *Foreign Policy Research Institute.* January 11. https://www.fpri.org/article/2021/01/does-africa-matter-to-the-united-states/.

Review, Michigan Technology Law, and Robert Kim. 2019. "Public Private Partnerships in National Cybersecurity." *Michigan Technology Law Review.* https://mttlr.org/2022/01/public-private-partnerships-in-national-cybersecurity/.

Roff, Peter. 2009. "Obama Wrong on D.C. School Vouchers and Hypocritical, Just Like Congress." *US News & World Report.* April 22. https://www.usnews.com/opinion/blogs/peter-roff/2009/04/22/obama-wrong-on-dc-school-vouchers-and-hypocritical-just-like-congress.

Rogin, Josh. 2010. "Mullen Goes to bat for State Department Budget." *Foreign Policy.* May 24. https://foreignpolicy.com/2010/05/24/mullen-goes-to-bat-for-state-department-budget/ .

Roos, Dave. 2021. "How John Marshall Expanded the Power of the Supreme Court." *History.* November 30. https://www.history.com/articles/supreme-court-power-john-marshall.

Roule, Norman. 2024. "American and the Middle East in 2025: Old Challenges, Broken Myths, New Opportunities." *Hoover Institution.* December 10. https://www.hoover.org/research/american-and-middle-east-2025-old-challenges-broken-myths-new-opportunities.

Saha, Devashree, Rajat Shrestha, Nate Hunt, and Evan Kim. 2024. "Navigating the EV Transition: 4 Emerging Impacts on Auto Manufacturing Jobs." *World Resources Institute.* June 13. https://www.wri.org/insights/ev-transition-auto-manufacturing-jobs.

Schmid, Hannah. 2023. "Chicago Public Schools dysfunction hits low-income, minority students." *Illinois Policy.* November 2. https://www.illinoispolicy.org/chicago-public-schools-dysfunction-hits-low-income-minority-students/.

Select Committee on Intelligence United States Senate. n.d. "Report on the U.S. Intelligence Community's Prewar Intelligence

Assessments on Iraq." https://irp.fas.org/congress/2004_rpt/ssci_concl.pdf.

Seshadri, Mallika. 2024. "LAUSD celebrates academic recovery, but a rough road lies ahead without Covid relief money ." *Ed Source*. October 11. https://edsource.org/2024/lausd-celebrates-academic-recovery-but-a-rough-road-lies-ahead-without-covid-relief-money/720504.

Sheiner, Louise, Lorae Stojanovic, and David Wessel. 2024. "How Does Medicare Work? And How is it Financed." *The Brookings Institute*. March 20. https://www.brookings.edu/articles/how-does-medicare-work-and-how-is-it-financed/.

Shivakumar, Sujai, Charles Wessner, and Thomas Howell. 2024. "Too Good to Lose: America's Stake in Intel." *Center for Strategic and International Studies*. November 12. https://www.csis.org/analysis/too-good-lose-americas-stake-intel#:~:text=According%20to%20a%20September%202024,yet%20ready%20for%20such%20production.

Smith, Jason. 2024. "Despite CBO's Predictions Trump Tax Cuts Were a Boom for America's Economy and Working Families." *U.S. House Committee on Ways and Means*. May 9. https://waysandmeans.house.gov/2024/05/09/despite-cbos-predictions-trump-tax-cuts-were-a-boon-for-americas-economy-and-working-families/.

Society of Professional Journalists. 2014. "SPJ Code of Ethics." *SPJ*. September 6. https://www.spj.org/spj-code-of-ethics/.

Solzhenitsyn, Alexandr. 1978. "A World Split Apart." *American Rhetoric Online Speech Bank*. June 8. https://www.americanrhetoric.com/speeches/alexandersolzhenitsynharvard.htm.

Spokojny, Dan. 2024. "Congressional Commission to Reform the State Department." *fp21*. September 30. https://www.fp21.org/publications/the-state-department-reform-commission.

Stein, Perry. 2022. "Literacy scores show widening achievement gap in D.C. during pandemic." *The Washington Post*. March 17.

https://www.washingtonpost.com/education/2022/03/17/dc-schools-achievement-gap-pandemic-reading/.

Stein, Ronald. 2024. "The Hydrocarbon Elephant in the room that Newsom Refuses to Address." *New Geography*. November 21. https://www.newgeography.com/content/007691-the-hydrocarbon-elephant-room-newsom-refuses-address.

—. 2024. "The Hydrocarbon Elephant in the Room that Newsom Refuses to Address." *New Geography*. November 21. https://www.newgeography.com/content/007691-the-hydrocarbon-elephant-room-newsom-refuses-address.

Swidershi, Tom, Sarah Crittenden-Fuller, and Kevin C. Bastian. 2024. "Student-Level Attendance Patterns Show Depth, Breath, and Persistence of Post-Pandemic Absenteeism." *The Brookings Institute*. September 9. https://www.brookings.edu/articles/student-level-attendance-patterns-show-depth-breadth-and-persistence-of-post-pandemic-absenteeism/.

The National Assessment of Educational Progress. 2022. *The Nation's Report Card*. Fall. https://www.nationsreportcard.gov/media.aspx.

TOI Staff. 2024. "Head of Iranian unit countering Mossad was Israeli agent, says ex-president Ahmadinejad." *The Times of Israel*. October 1. https://www.timesofisrael.com/head-of-iranian-unit-countering-mossad-was-israeli-agent-says-ex-president-ahmadinejad/.

Trujillo, Mariana. 2024. "California's State and Local Government Debt is over $500 Billion." *The Reason Foundation*. November 13. https://reason.org/commentary/californias-state-and-local-government-debt-is-over-500-billion/.

Turley, Jonathan. 2019. *Executive Privilege and Congressional Oversight*. May 15.

Turley, Jonathan. 2019. *The National Emergencies Act of 1976*. February 28.

U.S. Department of Defense. 2023. *2023 Cyber Strategy of the Department of Defense*. September 12. https://media.defense.

gov/2023/Sep/12/2003299076/-1/-1/1/2023_DOD_Cyber_
Strategy_Summary.PDF.

U.S. Government Accountability Office. 2024. *GAO.* December
17. https://www.gao.gov/products/gao-25-106749.

U.S. Naval War College Library. n.d. "Intelligence Studies: Types
of Intelligence Collection." *U.S. Naval War College Library.* https://
usnwc.libguides.com/c.php?g=494120&p=3381426.

Wackman, Thomas. 2023. "Energy Security is National Security."
Our Energy Policy. April 15. https://www.ourenergypolicy.org/
resources/energy-security-is-national-security/.

Wakabayashi, Daisuke, and Scott Shane. 2018. "Google will not
renew Pentagon contract that upset employees." *Business &
Human Rights Resource Center.* June 1. https://www.business-
humanrights.org/en/latest-news/google-will-not-renew-
pentagon-contract-that-upset-employees/.

Walters, Dan. 2024. "$165 Billion Revenue Error Continues to
Haunt the State." *Calmatters.* November 21. https://calmatters.
org/commentary/2024/11/california-state-budget-error/.

Walton, Robert. 2024. "AI, data center load could drive
'extraordinary' rise in US electricity bills: Bain analyst." *Utility
Dive.* October 23. https://www.utilitydive.com/news/data-center-
load-growth-us-electricity-bills-bain/730691/.

Wigfall, Catrin. 2024. "U.S. math scores decline dramatically on
international test." *American Experiment.* December 5. https://
www.americanexperiment.org/u-s-math-scores-decline-
dramatically-on-international-test/.

World Population Review. 2025. *Per Pupil Spending by State.*
https://worldpopulationreview.com/state-rankings/per-pupil-
spending-by-state.

Worldometer. 2024. "World / Countries / Iran." *Worldometer.* April
13. https://www.worldometers.info/coronavirus/country/iran/.

Yergin, Daniel. 2024. "US Energy Security: How We Got Here
and Where We Are Headed." *Hoover Institution.* September.

https://www.hoover.org/sites/default/files/research/docs/Yergin_
USEnergySecurity_web-240909.pdf.

Yingling, Paul. 2007. "A failure in generalship." *Armed Forces
Journal*. May 1. http://armedforcesjournal.com/a-failure-in-
generalship/.

Yoon, Julia. 2024. "Center for Strategic & International Studies."
Foreign-born Share of the U.S. STEM Workforce. April 5. https://
www.csis.org/analysis/innovation-lightbulb-foreign-born-share-
us-stem-workforce.

Zeya, Uzra, and Jon Finer. 2020. "Revitalizing the State
Department and American Diplomacy." *Council on Foreign
Relations*. November. https://www.cfr.org/report/revitalizing-
state-department-and-american-diplomacy.

Endnotes

1	(Hamre, et al. 2024)
2	(Blank 2023, Blank 2023)
3	(Bushnell 2021, Bushnell 2021)
4	(Bergmann, et al. 2024, Bergmann, et al. 2024)
5	(Kennan Institute 2024)
6	(Brzezinski 1997)
7	(Mullen 2011)
8	(R. Gates 2010)
9	(Center on Budget and Policy Priorities 2023)
10	(Sheiner, Stojanovic and Wessel 2024)
11	(Peck 2024)
12	(Walters 2024)
13	(Hernandez 2021)
14	(Trujillo 2024)
15	(Trujillo 2024)
16	(Hill 2024)
17	(Office of the New York State Comptrollers 2024)
18	(Smith 2024)
19	(McKay 2024)
20	(Shivakumar, Wessner and Howell 2024)
21	(Kotkin, America's Working Class is Back in Control 2024, Kotkin, America's Working Class is Back in Control 2024)
22	(Kotkin, Elon Musk and Woke Capital are in a Battle for the Future of America 2024)
23	(Kotkin, Elon Musk and Woke Capital are in a Battle for the Future of America 2024)
24	(Kotkin, Joel Kotkin: Western Nations Cripple their Economies with Green Initiatives While China and Others Laugh 2024)
25	(R. Stein, The Hydrocarbon Elephant in the room that Newsom Refuses to Address 2024)
26	(Musk and Ramaswamy 2024)
27	(Peter G. Perterson Foundation 2024)
28	(Swidershi, Crittenden-Fuller and Bastian 2024)
29	(Camera 2019)
30	(The National Assessment of Educational Progress 2022)
31	(Wigfall 2024, Project 2025 2023)
32	(Wigfall 2024)
33	(Bushnell 2021)

34	(Yoon 2024)
35	(Baron 2018)
36	(Yoon 2024)
37	(Kotkin, Why both sides are right in the H-1B visas row 2024)
38	(Anesta 2024)
39	(Anesta 2024)
40	(Office of the New York State Comptrollers 2024)
41	(Seshadri 2024)
42	(Papst 2024)
43	(Baltimore City Public Schools 2024)
44	(Roff 2009)
45	(Schmid 2023)
46	(Dabrowski and Klinger 2022)
47	(Grablick 2022)
48	(P. Stein 2022)
49	(World Population Review 2025)
50	(Center for an Informed Public University of Washington 2023)
51	(Hamre, et al. 2024)
52	(Peter G. Peterson Foundation 2024)
53	(Daniels 2024)
54	(Turley, Executive Privilege and Congressional Oversight 2019)
55	(Turley, The National Emergencies Act of 1976 2019)
56	(Ernst 2019)
57	(Musk and Ramaswamy 2024)
58	(First Liberty Institute 2024)
59	(Roos 2021)
60	(Hamilton 1788)
61	(Cordesman, Ending America's Grand Strategic Failures 2020)
62	(Hamre, et al. 2024)
63	(Cordesman, U.S. Military Spending: The Cost of Wars 2017)
64	(Society of Professional Journalists 2014)
65	(Solzhenitsyn 1978)
66	(Hanson 2025)
67	(Hanson 2025)
68	(Hanson 2025)
69	(Chivvis, et al. 2024)

70   (Spokojny 2024)
71   (Rogin 2010)
72   (R. M. Gates 2010)
73   (Zeya and Finer 2020)
74   (Patrick 2024)
75   (Okail and Duss 2024)
76   (Okail and Duss 2024)
77   (Clausewitz 1976)
78   (Churchill 1996)
79   (Chivvis, et al. 2024)
80   (Zeya and Finer 2020)
81   (Chambers II n.d.)
82   (Chodkowski 2012)
83   (Worldometer 2024)
84   (Zeya and Finer 2020)
85   (Project 2025 2023)
86   (Ledford 2024)
87   (Ledford 2024)
88   (Bruhl 2022)
89   (Bruhl 2022)
90   (Hughes 2013)
91   (Roule 2024)
92   (Roule 2024)
93   (Khan 2024)
94   (Khan 2024)
95   (Chivvis, et al. 2024)
96   (Kang and Lee 2024)
97   (Grabow 2019)
98   (Funaiole, et al. 2023)
99   (Kang and Lee 2024)
100   (Gunness and Saunders 2022)
101   (Cancian, Cancian and Heginbotham 2023)
102   (Haddick, Luria and Montgomery 2024)
103   (Jones 2024)
104   (O'Rourke 2024)
105   (Cordesman, Ending America's Grand Strategic Failures 2020)
106   (Cordesman, Ending America's Grand Strategic Failures 2020, Cordesman, The New Biden National Security 2022)
107   (Ochmanek, et al. 2023)
108   (Brown 2023)

109   (Brown 2023)

110   (Cordesman, Ending America's Grand Strategic Failures 2020)

111   (Davis 2013)

112   (U.S. Government Accountability Office 2024)

113   (Clark 2020)

114   (Clark 2020)

115   (Noonan 2024)

116   (Noonan 2024)

117   (Dickson 2020)

118   (Yingling 2007)

119   (Flickinger 2017)

120   (Garrity 2021)

121   (Devermont 2024)

122   (Devermont 2024)

123   (Devermont 2024)

124   (Kilcullen 2011)

125   (DeBatto 2020)

126   (U.S. Naval War College Library n.d.)

127   (Select Committee on Intelligence United States Senate n.d.)

128   (Moussa 2022)

129   (TOI Staff 2024)

130   (DeBatto 2020)

131   (Kirby and McKenzie Jr. 2021)

132   (DeBatto 2020)

133   (National Security Archive Electronic Briefing Book No. 207 2006)

134   (Marr, et al. 2008)

135   (Dunlop 2014)

136   (Dunlop 2014)

137   (Borshchevskaya 2021)

138   (Khvostunova 2024)

139   (Putin n.d.)

140   (Allison and Ferguson 2016)

141   (Bader 2016)

142   (Lellou 2024)

143   (Ray 2021)

144   (IN Homeland Security Staff 2012)

145   (Lynch 2022)

146   (Haugh 2024)

147   (Miller 2023)
148   (Barr 2020)
149   (Federal Bureau of Investigation 2019)
150   (Gilli and Gilli 2018/19)
151   (U.S. Department of Defense 2023)
152   (U.S. Department of Defense 2023)
153   (U.S. Department of Defense 2023)
154   (Morgan 2020)
155   (Ciphertex Data Security 2024)
156   (Review and Kim 2019)
157   (Haugh 2024)
158   (Ghaffary 2019)
159   (Wakabayashi and Shane 2018)
160   (Haugh 2024)
161   (Yergin 2024)
162   (Wackman 2023)
163   (Holtz-Eakin 2019)
164   (Wackman 2023)
165   (Lontay 2024)
166   (Lehr and Harris 2023)
167   (R. Stein, The Hydrocarbon Elephant in the Room that
        Newsom Refuses to Address 2024)
168   (Newsom 2020)
169   (Baskaran and Schwartz 2024)
170   (Bryce 2024)
171   (Wackman 2023)
172   (Institute for Energy Research 2018)
173   (Lasley 2018)
174   (Wackman 2023)
175   (Budinger 2024)
176   (Kotkin, Electric cars will decide the outcome of the
        American election 2024)
177   (Saha, et al. 2024)

Meet the Author

J ohn is a 30-year retired veteran of the United States Marine Corps with three combat tours in Iraq and Afghanistan. During his time in the Marine Corps, John has become a foremost authority on Civil Affairs as it relates to Counterinsurgency and Irregular Warfare and is an author in various military journals.

John served in Afghanistan in 2002, and 2012, and was deployed with the Marines in Ramadi, Iraq in 2005, where he conducted counterinsurgency and irregular warfare.

Currently, John is a bestselling author of a book published on Amazon titled, "The New Business Brigade: Veterans Dynamic Impact on U.S. Business." John also has had numerous articles published in national security journals and publications.

His knowledge of the Middle East region and national security policy has afforded him the opportunity to speak on many national and local news programs such as the syndicated national news program "Washington Journal" and other radio and television programs.

John is a frequent political commentator on various political news radio and television programs. Currently, John is a tri-weekly political commentator on WXJB-News Talk radio in the Tampa, Florida region.

John has a master's degree in National Security Studies from American Military University with a strong concentration in Middle Eastern Studies, and a bachelor's degree in government from California State University, Sacramento.

www.ingramcontent.com/pod-product-compliance
Lightning Source LLC
Chambersburg PA
CBHW060132100426
42744CB00007B/762